A Handful Of Prisms

Helene O'Shea

A Handful Of Prisms

Bedside Books
An imprint of American Book Publishing
American Book Publishing
P.O. Box 65624
Salt Lake City, UT 84165
www.american-book.com
Printed in the United States of America on acid-free paper.

A Handful Of Prisms

Designed by Kris Willhoite, design@american-book.com

Publisher's Note: *This is a work of fiction. Names, characters, places, and incidents either are the product of the author's imagination or, are used fictitiously, and any resemblance to actual persons, living or dead, events, or locales is entirely coincidental.*

Library of Congress Cataloging-in-Publication Data is available upon request.

ISBN 1-58982-161-0

O'Shea, Helene, A Handful Of Prisms

Special Sales

These books are available at special discounts for bulk purchases. Special editions, including personalized covers, excerpts of existing books, and corporate imprints, can be created in large quantities for special needs. For more information e-mail orders@american-book.com, 801-486-8639.

For my favorite generation:

Jeremy, David, Ryan, Garry, Michelle, Rosemary, Julianne, Matthew, Christopher, Grace, and Annmarie.

Foreword

I expected to enjoy this book, but I didn't expect to find it the most entertaining account of childhood I ever read.

Not exactly your run-of-the-mill childhood, certainly: a middle child of ten children living—and working as soon as they could start helping their parents—on a farm. Think of how much trouble an only child can get into if he or she tries, then multiply by ten, and you will have some idea of what can happen. Especially when several of them can draw on wild imagination and vast inexperience for group activity ideas.

Pop has a job in a store, with market gardening at home as his second job. Not surprisingly, he is a sourpuss. Mom is a treasure, an airhead one minute, full of common sense the next. The author does an enviable job of always telling the story from the children's viewpoint, especially her own, with constantly hilarious results.

Helene O'Shea spent several decades wishing she could write this memoir. Finally she has. It is worth the wait.

Scott Corbett

Scott Corbett is an award-winning author of many delightful children's books, but his greatest accomplishment is the love of reading he has instilled in two generations of children. He has published more than fifty books for children, as well as earlier books intended for an adult audience. The favorites at our house featured Kerby and Fenton and Mrs. Graymalkin in stories of fantasy skillfully interwoven with real life. If any Scott Corbett books are available on the market (I can never find any) they should be snapped up, as the next generation will enjoy them as certainly as the previous two have.

Helene O'Shea

Memory is a Prism

by
Helene O'Shea

Memory is the past set to music.
Drum rolls and Sousa marches for the
Brass-plated days of youth,
When everything was either possible or likely.
Silvery flute flights of notes
To mark the interment of stillborn dreams,
The realization of limitations.

Memory's pallet is smeared with pastels.
Muted tones.
The vivid purple of anger leached out
to insipid lavender.
The somber gray of depression
Touched with the shine of silver
From all those cloud linings.

Memory is a prism

Trapping and shattering the piercing light of grief
Into a myriad of multi-hues.
A refracted reflection
of gloom to joy.

Now is illusory, ephemeral;
Soon intangible, theoretical.
Then is all we have, the past recreated
In the recesses of ourselves.
Is happiness then reality?
Or just an illusion of sound and light?

Chapter One

The photograph albums were Laurel's idea and may have saved what sanity I had left after so many days bed-ridden. It's a phenomenon everybody has witnessed, how some ailments elicit instant sympathy whereas other ail-ments, just as painful or even more so, are considered fair game for the jokesters: summer colds, toothache, chicken pox. When you suffer from a broken hip, a mild heart at-tack, or a touch of arthritis, your friends are solicitous.

My visitors derived great mirth from my own predica-ment—trapped in traction, the great weight attached to my right leg pulling me irresistibly downward as I clutched at the bed sheets to keep from being jammed against the foot of the bed. And yet I needed their company badly enough to overlook their crude jests for the time being. When I was restored to a semblance of health, I would concoct some delicious revenge.

The box with the photo albums was dusty, and Laurel conscientiously wiped its surface with a damp cloth before lowering it awkwardly onto the flowered sheets. Those sheets were supposed to cheer me by lifting my mind outside my circumstances and into the sunshine of a spring day. They failed.

I lifted out the first photo album. Most of its black pages were dog-eared or torn, and the glue on corners in many instances framed nothing more than a darker area of page. *Aunt Sylvia,* the spidery white ink proclaimed below one such empty space where Aunt Sylvia's picture proved as transient as her several marriages.

"You always said when you had time you would organize these old pictures, and now you have all kinds of time." Laurel's eyes danced in her impish, freckled face, and she tried, entirely without success, to suppress a bubble of merriment. Maternity may have its rewards, but they do not include overmuch sympathy from teenaged daughters.

I dragged myself as nearly upright as the block and tackle allowed. My change of positions made the rope creak, the weight swing, and I had visions of going through what was left of life with one leg dragging elongated behind me like a bridal train.

I dug through the photographs that lay in handfuls in the bottom of the box. More were scattered between the layers of half-empty albums and scrunched in alongside—half a century of family life caught forever in awkward or self-conscious pose.

The top layers of photos were in the dying color of the beginner's instant camera, but beneath lay sepia-tones, intermixed with sharp black and white. Half a thousand pictures lay across my knees before I found the one that riveted my attention. Large, it would have covered an entire page of the book, with no room for the white script to name us. There we stood, my brothers and sisters, my parents, and I, caught for posterity, scowling or smirking into the camera, as our different personalities asserted themselves. We looked like a regiment, the twelve of us. No wonder we were never invited over for lunch.

Now I am oblivious to Laurel's mirthful look. I am transported back to that day—early November and we are not dressed for the breeze, no longer autumn playful, but vindictive, rushing around the corner of the house, skittering leaves from the great mulberry across the walk in front of us. The opening shutter has caught one just as it danced across my shoe, making it look as if I am standing at the edge of a small hole. Just for the moment, I no longer feel the pain of my recent problem or the pull of the doctor's sadistic contrivance. I am seven years old again, my rounded knees showing beneath my blue jumper and a quizzical smile on my lips as Uncle Freddy does his photographic stuff.

The picture was taken at a time dictated by the availability of the subjects. Carter wears his army-issued khaki and looks to be the only one of us not actually shivering. My sister Donley has a new plaid skirt made especially for the occasion; my own jumper was her last year's best outfit, now shortened, worked over to enhance me. The older boys—Conner, Trenton, and Lucas—slouch within heavy, plaid flannel shirts, and little Martin is resplendent in new corduroys and a hand-me-down sweater. It bags at the elbows and the waist because it is next to impossible to hem up or take in a sweater.

The locale of the photo, the side porch, was chosen because it had the advantage of needing only cursory tidying. An even greater advantage was the afternoon sunlight, which would make it unnecessary for Uncle Freddy to use flashbulbs, and this was a job for which payment would not be forthcoming.

There we all are. My father's outfit completed by a tie, over which he scowled his displeasure, the ten of us ranging in age from two to twenty, outfitted in dubious style, and my mother…for once her organizational ability had let her down and Uncle Freddy's arrival had found her in the dress she had worn all day. She wore a faded but charming print of violets that—I swear by all that's holy—had once been the sack for a hundred pounds of chicken feed. My sophisticated children find it hard to believe that during the '40s and '50s, one of the local feed companies had the bright idea to package their product in cotton prints which, when washed and ironed, became piece goods. What our wardrobes lacked in style, they more than made up for in color.

Uncle Freddy was in a hurry and had no time to sit with a piece of cake and a cup of coffee while Mother changed, so she solved the problem neatly by arranging herself on the broad, flat rail next to the steps where the rest of us posed, drawing baby Vala up close to her, hiding her own lack of finery. Her unstockinged legs were thrust sideways so that we children shielded her legs from sight. All that I see of her in the picture now is one sturdy arm clutching my baby sister, the sleeve of the violet-printed dress, and her gray-streaked hair framing her soft, smiling, exasperating, dear face. My eyes fill with tears, and I lie back on my bed of discomfort and give myself up to memory. Laurel tiptoes softly away.

Chapter Two

Grandmaw had, in the manner of her day, borne eight children, of whom only my mother, Jane, my Aunt Petty, and Uncle Freddy survived. I remember Grandmaw's parlor, the walls papered with elaborate specimens of botanical fantasy.

On the piano sat heavy tarnished silver frames, where the faces of those children who had not survived childhood looked out at the house they would never grow up in. Delicate Florence smiled, with no shadow of foreknowledge of the flu death that would claim her within ten months. Stocky Albert, pink of cheek (or so the re-touching made him seem) and defiant of glance, drowned at a church picnic, and infant Jeremiah was a victim of scarlet fever. Presumably the other two did not live long enough for the cameraman to be alerted.

Many a winter afternoon my sister Donley and I whiled away in Grandmaw's parlor, picking out notes on the piano, attempting to follow with neither talent nor instruction the wavering notes on the mountains of old sheet music. At lunchtime, Grandmaw reminisced about the three vanished members of her family, reiterated the sad story of the three separate tragedies, and lived again, this time tearlessly, through the three funerals. Donley and I, ghoulish little monsters, ate it up along with the homemade cottage cheese and the currant jelly bread.

The whole family was obsessed with names. A favorite subject over teacups between my Aunt Petty and mother was what reason Grandmaw had for naming them as she did. I don't know why they didn't simply ask her; it would have cut out a lot of repetitious conversation.

"Why couldn't I have been an entire flower?" Aunt Petty mourned. Until then, I had thought Petty to be a short form of Petronella. To find out that my aunt was "Petal" was a vast relief. And my mother, who was plainly named Jane, would smugly reply that it was infinitely preferable to Stem, for instance, or even Leaf. No matter how often my mother countered with this rejoinder, the two of them erupted in zany laughter. I feel sure that it was reaction to their dislike of their own names that made my mother and aunt choose to name their own children as they had. Had they known how often they would be called upon to find a suitable name, would they have ever launched themselves on the path they followed?

For Aunt Petty, who produced a child for every one of the ten my mother had—frequently within a month one way or the other of my mother's doing so—had chosen to give her children biblical names. Apparently the Old Testament had gone in heavily for "R's," for Aunt Petty's first three choices were Rachel, Rebecca, and Ruth. Then followed Joseph, Isaac, Benjamin, and Sarah, after which Aunt Petty eschewed the Old Testament to name her three youngest Elizabeth, Ann, and Mary. Her problems with the Good Book were eclipsed by the trouble my mother had, once she had set her foot on the path of family names, and was loathe to turn aside.

"Anyone can be Sue or Betty or Tom," she'd explain, thereby giving offense to any Sues, Bettys, or Toms, "but Carter Moss sounds important." Carter was her own maiden name.

Where Aunt Petty had innumerable books of the Bible from which to choose, even the most prolific family has only so many family names on the tree that adapt into a given name. Once when Carter and Conner were small, Mother took them with her to visit the cemetery and showed them the graves where their ancestors were buried. Pointing to one particular mound, she told Conner, "This is the relative you are named for."

Conner came home in tears and confided to his Grandmaw that he'd been named after a tombstone. Grandmaw dried his tears but couldn't help telling the story around, and we became known, even before I was born, as the Tombstone Kids. Some wit embellished on the name and called us the Mossy Tombstone Kids. Somehow the name did not appeal to my beleaguered mother.

Nonetheless, by assiduous research, Mother came up with enough family names for all of us. After Carter and Conner came Ragan, Carrington, Luke, Trenton, Donley, Odell (me), Martin, and Vala. Of course, it was hard to tell the players without a score card, and even to distinguish on the basis of first names if one were male or female. To eliminate confusion and placate the parish priest, who couldn't be talked into baptizing any children with such heathen names, Mother gave us each a second name. All the boys were Joseph; all the girls were Marie, thus: Carter Joseph, Conner Joseph, Ragan Marie, Carrington Marie, Lucas Joseph, Trenton Joseph, Donley Marie, Odell Marie, Martin Joseph, and Vala Marie. It's really easy when you understood the rules. We agreed among ourselves that Martin was the most fortunate. A lot of kids could be named Martin without any questions asked.

When I was very young, I noticed that my grandmother showed a strong preference toward me. At the time, I considered it just another indication of her good taste and sensitivity. Not until I entered first grade did it dawn on me one bright morning that my name was simply a derivative of Grandmaw's own maiden name, with the apostrophe and the capitol D left out of O'Dell. I came to terms early with the name because it was a link with my Grandmaw, but I never really cared for my nickname: Digger. Eventually my brothers and sisters dropped their use of it, but not until I was thirty years old.

Chapter Three

When I was in second grade and Donley in third, we shared the same classroom. There were only six classrooms at St. Albert's for eight grades, so somebody had to double up. It was fortunate that those nuns were such martinets, or Sister Mary Ellen would have had her hands full with twenty-two second graders and fourteen third graders.

It was a revelation to me to see a side of Donley that I was unfamiliar with. At home she blended into the crowd, but at school she was different. For one thing, she did her homework. Well, I did mine too, if it consisted of written-out arithmetic problems, because they collected those papers and there was trouble if you didn't turn yours in. On the other hand, when homework was studying spelling words, there was no way to prove you hadn't done the assignment, so I never did. Donley studied her spelling words and usually got them all right.

She was a gifted artist too. Scenes flowed from Donley's crayon like a cherished photograph. She could draw tree-studded hills with bright-colored kids on sleds slipping down, and you could almost see the passage of the breeze as they slithered past. Choirs of robed youths opened their collective mouths in song, and each one was an individual. You could all but hear the strains of the Easter music.

My range of recognizable art included Christmas trees—isosceles triangles, gold-star topped, with polka dots of red, purple, and gold to represent ornaments. My other specialty was angels: haloed heads, flowing garment, and wings. I also did tulips: stiff stems rising from a bowl with the U-shaped flowers in three colors. Sometimes I put a daisy within the bouquet, but I am not certain that is botanically sound, since when tulips bloom, the daisies are still lurking sullenly underground.

Fortunately for me, art was a semi-occasional class, its schedule dictated by whim. Late in January, Sister Mary Ellen passed out the heavy manila-colored paper, which signified art class was about to begin, and invited us to design a Valentine.

I gnawed on my crayons awhile and then drew an angel—well, I'd used the Christmas tree for the previous art lesson. It was one of my better efforts, I thought, and I added carefully printed wording: "Valentines are angelic." I decided that I had outdone myself. I made an excuse to take myself to the aisle where Donley's desk was, and there on her manila paper was a Cupid, complete with quiver of arrows and a drawn bow, aiming at a lacey heart. It was perfect. Even though she had, like me, only one sheet of art paper and nothing on which to practice. If they graded on the curve, I was going to fail art class once again.

Chapter Three

It was worse than that. Sister Mary Ellen made fun of my effort.

"Odell, what is this? What do angels have to do with Valentine's Day?"

I wanted to say that February 14 was the saint's day for St. Valentine and had religious foundations, but I thought as a religious person she should know that. I didn't though, because seven-year-olds did not talk back to nuns or they would be referred to as "bold little lassies," the worst comment the sisters allowed themselves to use in public. So I sat there silently and took the verbal abuse, thinking that I should have used the tulip drawing I was capable of but I wanted to save that one for Easter.

I was even more humiliated when Sister held up Isobel Gordon's work and compared it to mine, much to my discredit. It is possible that Isobel was not the envy of the entire second grade, but she certainly was an object of my envy. She was exquisite from her geometrically perfect long, black curls to the bottoms of her white strap sandals. Her appearance gave her a confidence most second graders never know. Isobel had drawn a lopsided kitten, wild-eyed and whiskered, and added the phrase, "I would purr if you would be my Velantine." The child couldn't even spell, I told myself with condescension, and I hated her and Sister Mary Ellen with equal ferocity.

Next day Sister designed the Valentine Box with Donley's help. She covered the whole thing with white construction paper, and had Donley cut out silhouettes of her Cupid to paste on the side, along with copies of Donley's lacy hearts, and they added ribbons of crepe paper at the corners to flutter in the breeze from the air duct. Altogether, the Valentine Box was a thing of beauty and a joy to little kids. If I hadn't been so angry with Sister Mary Ellen, I might have actually enjoyed it.

Donley, though, was enthusiastic and excited until Sister handed out the list, smudged from the copier, with the name of everybody in the class so we would know how to spell all the names, since she expected we would send a valentine to each and every kid in our class.

"Hey Digger ," she asked with worry in her voice, on the way home from school. " Do you think Sister expects us to send valentines to everybody?"

Yes, I thought she expected that. She probably wanted me to include Isobel, who couldn't even spell the word.

"What do you think Mother will say?" Donley asked.

What Mother said, looking up from the last of the autumn carrots she was peeling, was "I bought valentines today." With a movement of her chin, she indicated the package on the kitchen table.

"25 Valentines 25," it said across the front and again at the side. "25 Valent…" The package was torn.

"Somebody opened my valentines," Donley said.

"Not your valentines," Mother said. "I bought the package for you to share."

Share? Twenty-five valentines when Donley needed thirty-six. She'd done her homework well enough to know that you had to add to twenty-five to get thirty-six, not divide. But Martin and Vala had already removed their favorites from the package. They'd taken six each. Donley looked at me over the remaining thirteen valentines.

"You can have mine, Donley," I promised. After all, hadn't she helped hide the pieces when I accidentally broke my pop's favorite coffee cup? Hadn't she shown me how to use the heavy twine from the barn to replace a broken shoelace? Wasn't I now soured on the whole idea, having had my feelings hurt by my teacher?

Donley was still twenty-two valentines short. She approached Martin to deal with him. What did he need with valentines? He didn't go to school, and he certainly wasn't going to be given postage stamps with which to mail his cards.

"What will you take for your valentines, Martin?" Donley asked gently.

Martin's face was smeared with chocolate, and his sweet smile was even sweeter than usual due to the chocolate on his teeth. He would trade his slightly used valentines for Donley's supper dessert of chocolate pudding. Poor Donley liked chocolate as well as anybody, but she felt some kind of responsibility to the valentine box she helped to create, and she made the trade. One of Martin's valentines was missing a head, but judicious use of scotch tape took care of that, and a facecloth gently applied removed most of the chocolate from yet another.

Vala was a different story. "No," she said before Donley could open her mouth. "I want all my valentines."

But in the end, she agreed that if Donley would hand over all the valentines she received, Vala would surrender all she presently had. The child obviously knew about trading in futures.

So there was Donley with twenty-five valentines to spread among thirty-six people. Or rather thirty-five, since she need not send one to herself. Maybe she could eliminate all the second graders, but what would be thought of her if she were to skip her own sister? In the little bedroom under the eaves, which we shared, I knew Donley scarcely slept that night.

When we got to school the next morning, there was Isobel, her pink flowered dress matched by her extravagant hair ribbon and her socks, divesting herself of her valentines. One by one she dropped them into the box. Encased in large white envelopes, they were clearly a higher art form than was afforded by 25 Valentines 25. Well, that was what you'd expect of Isobel, but then another girl and another girl and then a boy approached and shoveled envelope after envelope into the beautiful valentine box. Shortly afterward, the teacher announced that anybody else with valentines should place them temporarily on the corner of her desk, since the box was full.

At lunch, Donley confided that she had not put her valentines on the desk. What if the teacher recognized her handwriting and counted only as far as 25 and knew that Donley didn't have cards for everybody? Her anxiety was beginning to have its effect on me. After all, I didn't have any valentines at all, and my bravado was beginning to deteriorate.

That afternoon, Sister brought a brand new wastebasket from the store room and within minutes, with more construction paper and crepe paper, created another vision of beauty: a Valentine Wastebasket. She explained that the overflow of greeting cards could be contained within its loveliness. None of us felt the least bit slighted to have our valentines put into the wastebasket. Still, Donley did not approach to add her valentines to the container.

We had trotted almost halfway home from school when Donley admitted that she had waited all day for a private moment to take care of the cards she had secreted in the depths of her desk and had never found the proper time. Now she was frightened that she would get sick tomorrow, and somebody would go through her desk in her absence and discover her lack of cards for the whole class.

"Let's go back," I said. "Nobody will see us put the valentines in now."

So, even though we knew we would be late getting home and have to find an explanation, we trotted all the way back. Back into the classroom like a flash, Donley searched her desk, found the valentines, and was approaching the front of the room when she saw Mr. Glass, the janitor, leaning on his broom and grinning at her. He was standing in front of the valentine wastebasket, and Donley did not like to ask him to move.

"That's a lot of valentines for one little girl," he said. "When I was young, I never sent more than one, sometimes two valentines." He wasn't' being sarcastic; his voice held nothing but nostalgia. "You must be a very popular little girl to have that many friends."

Poor Donley wept and the whole story came out: the valentine box, the list from the teacher, the valentines she had managed to get, her feeling of not living up to expectations, her worry that some kids would be implacable enemies because of having been left off her list.

Mr. Glass reached out a gnarled hand and took the valentines. Reaching up, he thrust them into the decorated box, and shook his head.

"That's not what valentines are about. You send valentines to the people who mean something to you or they don't mean anything at all. It's a fearful shame."

We got out of there.

Next morning, I wouldn't look directly at the box. My eyes slewed sideways to take it in and noticed something amiss. The valentine wastebasket was no longer in the spot where I had seen it as recently as last night after school.

Our teacher was visibly upset. She faced the classroom and announced in a somber voice worthy of a funeral oration. "Children, I have very bad news."

I held my breath to the point of dizziness. Had she found us out? Was she prepared to announce to the class that between the two Moss children, less than 30 valentines were being sent? No.

"Last night Mr. Glass cleaned our classroom and emptied our valentine wastebasket into the incinerator. Half our valentines have been burned up," she said. "Mr. Glass said he did not notice that the basket was decorated or full of unopened envelopes. He said a wastebasket was just that, and it is his job to empty it." She wasn't all that happy with Mr. Glass.

So we opened the valentine box and distributed what was in there, including all Donley's valentines. Nobody voiced any regret about the limited number of valentines they received, except for Isobel. Her voice could be heard across the two rows that separated her from my seat.

"And all because of Mr. Glass, I got only 18 valentines when I would have had 36."

I thought about what Grandmaw used to say, "What the mind doesn't know, the heart doesn't grieve over."

With her worries lifted away, Donley really seemed to enjoy her cookies and lemonade, which were the Valentine treat. We were so light-hearted that we almost danced home that afternoon.

Donley and I never knew whether Mr. Glass had done that on purpose or not. Still, when he retired after that school year and a collection was taken up for him, we emptied our meager piggy bank savings and donated it all to the cause.

Chapter Four

On a rainy day in June, my sister Carrington, aided and abetted by cousin Ruth, her opposite number from Aunt Petty's family, devised a play. We couldn't hope for much in the way of an audience, but Grandmaw and Grandpaw, Mom and Pop, Aunt Petty, and Uncle Mathew had promised to attend. Not only was admission free, but by pooling our funds we had managed to buy an entire carton of six bottles of soft drink. This was to be offered as refreshment while the play was performed. That way, since the entire younger generation could be expected to be actually onstage or in the wings awaiting their cue to present themselves, there was no need to offer them a share. It was just as well that we knew no more than six adults were to attend, since a seventh would have been forced to go embarrassingly unrefreshed.

With the soft drinks on ice, we closed off Grandmaw's double parlor and began rehearsal. I wasn't all that impressed with the main body of the play, since I wasn't allowed a part in it. I sat and sulked while my elders donned long dresses and bonnets acquired in a raid on Grandmaw's attic.

"But just wait," my cousin Ruth soothed, "when we get to your part, you'll really like it."

I smiled and prepared to be in a better mood. Ruth, with her dark hair and dimples, could charm the birds from the trees or a pout from a small cousin. I watched the action on stage for awhile, but I never did comprehend the plot. It was hidden beneath flourishes of long, ruffled skirts and curtseys elaborately performed. There was also a good deal of sweeping off of hats, particularly by those actors fortunate enough to have been outfitted with plumes in their hat bands. Finally it was my turn for dress rehearsal.

My little part was intended to divert the audience while the scene was changed between acts. Dressed in my best dress—a lavender organdy in which I very much admired myself—I was to stand at the very edge of the area designated as the stage and, holding two of Grandmaw's tea roses to my shoulders, I was to recite a perfectly sickening little verse: "I have roses on my shoulders."

The stage direction for this line was to toss my two rosebuds into my admiring audience.

"I have slippers on my feet." *Hold up a patent leather-clad foot* (the stage direction read), which, sad to say, was badly scuffed since I wasn't the first kid to wear these shoes.

"I'm Mother's little darling." *Wide smile.*

"Don't you think I'm sweet?" *Coy looks and wait for applause.*

Chapter Four

I was absolutely appalled. Perhaps I couldn't throw a football so that it came to earth in a perfect spiral nor could I be trusted not to drown in ten feet of water, but that didn't mean I had to make an utter fool of myself.

Even Ruth was not able to persuade me, though she dimpled prettily and kissed me and told my sister Carrington that I was not a spoiled rotten brat; I simply had a serious case of stage fright. Sweet words fell on deaf ears, along with threats of bodily harm and worse: exclusion from the daily baseball games. I remained unwavering.

Finally, Carrington hit on a threat that would ordinarily have moved me. She would groom Vala for my part. On any other occasion, Carrington would have been absolutely correct. My envy of Vala as baby and pet knew no bounds, at least until the time of the play. When they went out of the parlor and returned with my littlest sister, I knew my first pang of sympathy for her since they had brought her home from the hospital three years ago.

Vala was not a quick study. Even when Ruth removed all the thorns from the beginning-to-wither rosebuds, she was still not sure she wanted to hold them. Nor, at three, was she able to learn four entire lines of poetry. She would need a prompter.

While Ruth arranged the chairs for the expected audience, Carrington dragged baby Vala out of the room to see what changes could be made to improve her appearance, so that she would be more easily accepted in the role of Mother's little darling. I could have told them no change was necessary. Sunday-dressed or covered with mud, Vala was, had been, and would always be Mother's little darling since the day she made her first appearance in our lives. It was a role she carried superbly.

"You know"—Ruth's voice was honey sweet, a tone she never used to her own younger sisters and brothers—"if you don't do this poem, Odell, you won't be in the play at all. I sure don't want to have a play without including you."

I didn't answer. I was too busy wondering if being a member of the audience meant I would be served refreshments.

Ruth continued to wheedle until the curtain was ready to open, forty minutes late. Just before the audience was allowed into the theatre, she must have realized that I was immutable, because she kicked me sharply in the shin and tried to rush me out of the room, revealing her true colors. That was the way she generally treated my cousins. The dimples and dark curls disguised an older sister every bit as mean as my own.

I knew when I wasn't wanted, and I wouldn't stay where I wasn't welcome. Grandmaw's back bedroom shared a closet with the parlor, an eight-foot square space divided by a flimsy board, so that bedroom clothing hung on the bedroom side and the coats and hats of visitors hung on the parlor side. I entered the closet, crept under the short partition, and emerged on the other side.

I opened the closet door wide enough to give me a glimpse of the stage. Luckily, the audience half of the room was dimmed with the drapes pulled and the lamps unlit. The stage area was brightened by the simple expedient of laying a floor lamp on its side, indicating how good a sport Grandmaw was, and draping some dark cloth around the audience side of the lampshade and sending all light toward the stage.

By the time I got settled, the first act of the play was just ending. It was a very short play. Perhaps we had no confidence in our ability to rivet an audience. Carrington and Ruth, who had the leads since they had written and directed the whole thing, stood hand-in-hand at the very edge of the lighted area and queried the audience.

"What can we two young girls do to save our father from bankruptcy?"

Instead of an answer, they got Trenton and Isaac pulling a sheet across in front of their noses, signaling the audience that if they wanted to know, they would have to stay tuned.

Vala made her appearance, coming through the drawn sheet-curtain and standing silently, allowing the audience a quiet moment to admire her costume. From Grandmaw's reserves of material, Carrington had unearthed a length of blue, silky material, and this was wound, sari fashion, around Vala's small chubby body. A large blue ribbon had been tied around her head to hide her wispy blonde hair, which refused any disciplining.

The pause lengthened, and Vala looked to her left and right, her chubby fingers crushing her two tired rosebuds to her shoulders.

Eerily, into the darkness came Carrington's voice: "I have roses on my shoulders," and Vala's trembling squeak echoed: "I have woses on my showders."

Carrington could not have realized how loud her voice was: "Slippers on my feet." And "Slippers on my feet," responded Vala.

The audience was beginning to murmur among its half-dozen selves, particularly my mother and Aunt Petty, who were disposed to laughter when they occupied the same room. As they finished the last two lines and Vala released her rosebuds on schedule into her admiring audience, the voice of my brother Trent could be heard. "Yeah, Carrington, we sure do think you're sweet."

His effort to mimic Vala was not really successful, but close enough to start me giggling as I crouched hidden behind the barely opened closet door. Picturing Carrington's indignation and encouraged by the occasional muffled snort from the recognized audience, I was rocked so hard by my own amusement that I fell forward against the closet door. It swung wide open, crashing against a table that had been moved to allow the audience's chairs to be properly lined up and on which a tray containing the refreshments had been left. Someone had the idea of uncapping the soft drink bottles and pouring them into Grandmaw's fanciest glasses. I'll bet it was Ruth—it was just like her. The idea proved to be a really rotten one, for table, tray, glasses, and most regrettable of all—cola—went crashing.

Only one of Grandmaw's good glasses failed to survive, but a high-flying glass spilled its contents onto the overturned lamp with predictable results: a flash of light and then dusk in the afternoon. The daylight could not penetrate Gram's velvet drapes. Uncle Matthew and my pop rose hurriedly to find new fuses to repair the damage, and Grandmaw hastily unplugged the lamp lest the new fuse go the way of the old. They opened drapes to admit light and cleaned up the mess, and with one thing and another the performance was not resumed.

Neither Carrington nor Ruth spoke to me for the rest of the day. I considered their ostracism of me to be totally unfounded. After all, if Trent hadn't said what he did, or if Carrington hadn't spoken so loudly as prompter, or if Ruth hadn't written such stupid lines for us to recite, none of it would have happened. And furthermore, had their old play been as good as they thought it was, wouldn't the grown-ups have been anxious, once things were righted, to see the rest? But of course, since they no longer had refreshments to look forward to, perhaps they thought it better to cut their losses.

We left Grandmaw's house soon after, and we all found places in the car. With only a roomy sedan and ten youngsters to fit within it, Pop could have given lessons to a sardine canner. Pop started to remonstrate with me for my carelessness, my irresponsibility, and my lack of good manners. Sitting perched on the lap of one of my older sisters, I hung my head, less in shame than in chagrin. I had already worked out in my mind why only a small particle of blame for the fiasco should have been mine. Halfway home, it occurred to me that at no time during his scolding had my father actually looked at me or called me by name. Of course, given the number of his children, he might be having trouble recalling my name, but surely he might have glanced my direction to see how repentant I was. As we shuffled inside from the car, Donley preceded me, and my father gave her a resounding smack across the bottom to teach her to behave herself better on the next occasion, supposing there to be another. Just as I thought. Despite the fact that slender Donley was several inches taller than I, had light blonde hair to compare to my no-color hair, my father couldn't tell us apart.

I wonder how many swats and lectures she received over the years that should have been directed my way. I guess since she was no angel either, perhaps things evened out in the long run.

Chapter Five

I would have been clean away except for the squeaky hinge on the front door. It always alerted my mother where she sat sewing in the front room.

"Take Vala with you. She needs a little fresh air."

Good grief! She hadn't even come out of the room, not even to the doorway, to see who she was giving the order to. For all she knew, I might have been some foul kidnapper rashly poking my head through an unlocked door to see what pickings were available.

For the space of a long breath, I debated easing on out the door and pretending I hadn't heard. I could always deny later that it was I who had been leaving, but as if my mother sensed my embryo rebellion, she called out more loudly, "Do you hear me, Odell? Take the baby out with you."

It reinforced my long-held belief that the worst place to be born was in the middle of a big family. I was perfectly sure that when I had been Vala's age, no one had been commanded to share his or her playtime with me. I was probably incarcerated in the heavy old crib through most of the day until I learned to fend for myself. Probably I was five or six years old before I ever saw the sunshine.

I shed a few tears over the picture of my sickly three-year-old self and seized Vala's mittened hand roughly. I all but dragged her down the high porch stairs, careful to avoid being seen from the window where my mother sat. My mother wielded a wickedly accurate hairbrush, and I didn't want to arouse her ire.

It was cold, but not so cold as it had been all week. The sun was even now melting the last of the Christmas snow, and only on the north of the house and in the shadow of each brick step was any snow left in quantities large enough to fashion a snowball. Vala, clumsy in her snowsuit and oversize galoshes—they had been mine until last year, and must have been at least three sizes too big for the baby's feet—stumbled and fell in her attempt to keep up with me.

We were heading down the hill to the place where a wooden bridge spanned the ice-slowed stream. I could see Trent and Donley far in front of me. They had cleverly managed to leave the house unencumbered by our little sister. I shouted and waved, and they responded with shouts and waves that meant for me to hurry. Trent was carrying a gunnysack, and I knew what our plans for the day were, and that it would have been far, far better if Vala had not had to be included.

"What'd you bring her along for?"

Chapter Five

Trenton's voice was rife with scorn, but he knew very well why I had brought Vala. He'd been bright enough to escape through the rear door carrying the kitchen wastebasket. If I had looked, I could have seen it standing alongside the burn barrel, abandoned. Bright as she indubitably was, our mother had never suspected anything when Trenton donned mittens, galoshes, and earmuffs to take the garbage out.

"Whatcha got in the sack, Trenton?"

For a wonder, Vala exhibited no traumatic or psychological effects of being constantly unwanted by her older siblings. Trenton unwisely opened the neck of the sack and showed her. It was unwise because Vala tattled, sometimes inadvertently and sometimes with the sole purpose of making trouble for somebody. Sometimes to entertain, sometimes innocently, but sooner or later, she told. Her mouth was a force to be reckoned with.

"Dollies!" she said now, peering into the sack.

Sure enough, Trent's burden was four dollies, two of mine, two of Donley's.

Every Christmas, Donley and I could count on at least two dollies, mostly the baby doll variety, cloth of body, rubber of legs, with a lovely, simpering face created of some non-waterproof composite. Aunt Petty chose a dolly for each of us with loving care, and with greater love, dressed them in beautiful gingham dresses far nicer than anything in Donley's or my own wardrobe. For as long as I could remember, there had been a big gaudily papered package under the tree for my sister and me, which predictably contained yet another doll. Add to that the predilection of another aunt—our father's sister—to gift us on occasion with a dolly. What, after all, could be more desirable for two young girls?

It was easy to agree with Trent's assessment that we would be up to our asses in dollies if we didn't take steps. And this morning, those steps lay away from the house and down to the stream, where, after Trent used a knife purloined from the kitchen to cut out the mechanism that made the babies cry, we set the dollies, one by one, to float in the stream until their cloth bodies became water-soaked and they sank to a watery death. It provided an entire day's entertainment. We gleaned another whole hour's diversion when we buried all the dollies in four pathetic little graves scooped out of the ground and marked their last resting-places with crosses fashioned from lilac twigs. Satisfyingly mournful.

I thought of those new dollies even now resting on mine and Donley's bed. Aunt Petty's donations were dressed in yellow and white checks with panties and bonnet to match and cleverly contrived socks and shoes adorning their hard rubber feet. The other dollies had been given to us by our parents and were identical in their pink organdy and golden curls framing their bright eyes. Within twelve months, their eyes would dim, their curls mat into a veritable forest of tangles, the pink organdy (or yellow gingham) hang limp, and they would be ready to follow their predecessors. *Sic Transit Gloria Mundi*!

If Mother ever wondered about the fate of the old dollies, she never did so aloud in our presence, but allowing

Vala to witness their timely end would assuredly bring down our mother's wrath on the dolly executioners.

Trent came up with a solution—Trent was famous for his solutions. Not far from the bridge from which we allowed each dolly in turn to seek oblivion and the hereafter stood an oversized doghouse, once the home of the legendary Betsy, hunting dog extraordinaire. Betsy had been dispatched from this mortal coil by a bullet from the gun of a rabbit hunter who had overdone the anti-freeze in the flask he carried. She was much mourned by my father, who despaired of ever being able to replace her. I didn't envy the dog her place in my father's affections, but I did envy her the name Betsy. Who ever heard of giving a dog a person's name and giving children the kind of names we all sported?

"We're playing bloodhound, Vala." Trenton was very convincing. Even I began to wonder if the day's plans had undergone a change. "These poor dollies are going to be lost in the woods."

Trent swung a hand out in a wide gesture to encompass the high weeds along the railroad track that backed the field, as well as the winter-bare willows growing along the stream.

"Donley, Digger, and I are a search team, and we're going to hunt and hunt for these dollies, but we're not going to find them."

The more he talked, the more it became evident that Trent's career could easily include successful selling, possibly used cars.

"That's where you come in. You get to be the bloodhound!"

Vala's eyes shone as if Trent were promising her butterscotch pudding. She clapped her small hands within her oversized mittens and jumped a time or two for joy, her boots remaining motionless on the hard ground.

"You'll have to wait, though, while we conduct a search with the available manpower," Trent explained. "Nobody ever gets the bloodhounds out of their kennels until they have exhausted every other means."

Vala's face became suitably grave as Trenton led her back a few feet to the abandoned, kennel.

Obviously, Betsy had been a larger species than poor Vala, for the toddler had room to spare in the doghouse.

"I'll wait right here," she promised Trenton, looking up adoringly.

He should have been ashamed of himself. If Vala had ever cast that trusting look up at me, I would never have been able to take advantage of her innocent youth. But Vala was a man's girl, and Trent was just a young boy.

Although it was months after Betsy's demise, there was still an aura and redolence of dog about the kennel, but Vala either didn't notice or didn't care, with her imagination captured by the next exciting move. Trenton magnanimously dumped the dollies from the gunnysack and allowed Vala to use it to carpet the floor of the kennel so that she need not squat on the cold ground.

"But I guess I should put the dog collar on you, Val, just for atmosphere."

Poor Vala suffered herself to be collared, not around her small neck, but at the waist, with the buckle of the collar at her back beneath her heavy jacket. She offered a series of dog noises: bow wows, grrs, ruff-ruffs, and snapped her teeth.

Gathering up the dollies, we headed for the stream, Trent warning us that we better not linger overmuch at our game, since Vala was nothing if not impatient. And honestly, we didn't intend to. But it was Christmas vacation from school on a glorious winter day, so far a bit milder than usual. And we were having fun.

None of us children owned a watch—it was unheard of in those days for any child to have one—but eventually after much drama over the death of each dolly in turn, we noticed the sun had traveled a good long way since we arrived at the stream, and we were getting very cold. Trenton had injudiciously allowed slivers of ice to slide into his boots, and his feet, he now announced, were freezing. Both Donley and I had dampened our mittens, and our fingers felt like the chunks of ice we had broken from the banks of the stream in our unavailing efforts to succor each drowned dolly. It was more than time to go back in the house. And then we remembered Vala.

She had cried herself out fairly early, but spunky child that she was, found a new supply of tears and screams to greet us as we emerged from behind a clump of willows and started the uphill trot to her doghouse.

"You didn't mean to come get me at all," she screamed at Trenton and delivered a kick on his shin, a kick that lost its impetus when her small foot slipped from the loose embrace of her overlarge galoshes. The galosh flew through the air and landed harmlessly behind us.

"You meant to just leave me here in this smelly old doghouse while you played."

Naturally, we denied it. Of course, we had intended to leave her there, but it would hardly have been politic to admit it, and certainly leaving her this long was simply a matter of acoustical accident. If the willows and the weeds had not been so thick that they muted her cries of distress, we would never have forgotten her presence for such a long period of time. We hastened to assure her, our feet displaying symptoms of incipient frostbite, possibly gangrene.

"We were just on our way to get you. Heck, you thought it was hours I bet, but it just proves how time goes slow when you're anxious." But Trenton was not allowed to continue his philosophical discourse.

"You're plain wicked, Trenton. And Donley and Odell too." And then she delivered her coup de grace: "I'm gonna tell on you." And she would too, she would.

We gazed at the legendary tattletale, then exchanged guilty looks among ourselves. I opened my mouth to speak but thought better of it. The only idea I could think of was to send her downstream in imitation of our late, unlamented dollies, but to speak the thought aloud would simply give Vala more ammunition for her mouth.

"Silly Vala!" Trent was again the fastest thinker. "Let me get you loose from the doghouse. See, I'll have to keep you on the lead so we can follow you into the woods and find the dollies."

But Vala had lost all sympathies for lost dollies. She presumed them dead and refused to be captivated again by the promise of sharing in the bloodhound game. She stamped her stocking foot and demanded to be taken back to the house. She was hungry. She also smelled rather bad, but again I thought better than to mention it.

"Okay, we'll play another game." Trenton winked at me in a signal for me to go along with whatever he thought of, but at this point, my feet were joining my hands in crystallizing into ice forms, and I was ready to take my punishment in order to get warm. Nevertheless, loyalty was loyalty, blood was thicker, if no warmer, than water, and I knew I would follow his lead.

Trenton took Vala several feet away from me, and he and Donley whispered to her, and whatever they were saying seemed to please her mightily. She nodded her head with enthusiasm, allowed Donley to shove the galosh abandoned a few minutes ago over her foot, and led the way quite merrily back to the stream.

I followed with less enthusiasm and found when I pushed my way through the hanging fronds of willow that Trenton had built an auxiliary bridge across the water using a few rocks and a plank of wood left lying there from one of last summer's games.

"We're going to play Billy Goat Gruff," he called to me, and I wondered how he could muster up so much loud, if insincere, camaraderie. I was cold.

"Okay, I'll be the big billy goat, Donley will be the middle billy goat, and Digger can be the little billy goat. Vala, you get to be the troll under the bridge."

Troll, indeed, I thought. If it weren't for Vala's unforgiving and malignant nature, we would all be huddled around the heating stove in the living room.

Vala knelt on the bank of the stream, guarding the footpath that led to the bridge, as nearly like the old fairy tale as we could manage on such short notice.

"Here I go across the bridge…I'm the big billy goat gruff."

If Vala had some lines to say, she neglected to come in on cue, as Trenton tromped loudly across the plank. "Now you, Donley."

"I'm the middle billy goat gruff," she said.

I should have picked up on the subdued note in the voice of the middle-sized billy goat gruff. Donley was my unwavering ally, and she was unhappy about what was coming.

"Okay," I muttered half under my breath. "Anything to get this over with." I stepped a foot on the plank and started across. "I'm the littlest billy…"

My darling little sister used the stout stick that my trusted brother gave her to upturn the plank, and I lost my balance, exactly as planned, and fell face first into three feet of icy water in the shallow creek bed.

At first I was too stunned to realize what had happened, but the eddies of water and slush around my nose brought me quickly to my senses and my feet.

"Doggone it, Vala, what do you think you are doing?"

But Vala was collapsing with laughter at the success of the scheme Trent had devised to divert her mind from tattling. Forgotten now was the long, cold wait in the bloodhound kennel and the demands of her stomach to be fed. Vala was happy as a hog on ice, to use a particularly appropriate simile. There was something basically nasty about that child.

"I had to do it, Digger." Trenton was now sincerely regretful. "If I hadn't thought up something like this, she would have told Mom and Pop we tied her up in the doghouse, and now she can't tell, because she's done something worse."

I wanted to tell Trent that I wasn't impressed with his machinations, but my teeth were chattering too hard. Whatever Vala had told, no punishment Mother devised could be worse than what I was suffering now.

But even for this predicament, Trenton had a solution. Quick as a rat, for a mouse was too innocent an animal, he scrambled up the slope to the kennel to wrap my damp shoulders in the meager warmth of the burlap bag. His arm around me, coaxing me forward, my brother indicated that I should take shelter from the cold winds of the day in the equally meager shelter of the doghouse. And at this point, I was willing to overlook the lingering Betsy-scent.

"You girls stay here," he directed, "and I'll run up to the house and get Odell something dry and warm to put on." And good as his word, he was away in a burst of speed.

The water dripping off my body did nothing for the aura of my temporary shelter. It was as if the remnants of Betsy had been dehydrated, and it took only the addition of the water I was providing to bring them back to their original smelly existence. Donley crouched as close to the entrance of the doghouse as her sense of smell would allow, thinking to shield me from the wind, but also denying me the comfort of clean fresh air.

Vala was soon bored and wandered off in Trent's path, making her blameless way back to the house.

It seemed like hours. I remembered Trent explaining to Vala about the expanding qualities of time and admitted that he might be right.

"I came as fast as I could," Trent said, thrusting an old coat, grabbed rather than chosen, from the many pegs in the back hall, into the opening of the doghouse. The baloney sandwich in his mouth indicated to me that he hadn't given my predicament first priority. "Phew! Sheesh!" said my brother, my co-conspirator, my savior. "You really stink!"

I wrapped the coat around me and headed homeward with my teeth still clicking and my feet unable to decide between rapid movement, which caused the wind to flurry around and find openings in the old coat, and slow movement, which allowed the cold greater time to freeze my blood where it slushed through my veins.

When we had gained the house, there was Mother blocking the back porch, against all odds, when I had hoped to sneak through it and via the basement to dry clothing.

"What happened, Odell?"

She led us all in to the blessed warmth of the kitchen where the soup kettle on the stove emitted an aroma to vie with that of the fresh-baked bread on the table, both smells utterly routed by my own noxious odor. Vala sat in the high chair she had long since outgrown. Her legs hung far past the ledge intended for the feet of a younger child, but she clung to the chair, possibly to enhance and advertise her position as baby of the family. That kid knew which side her bread was buttered on, and right now it was the heel of the loaf—the favored slice—into which she was sinking her teeth.

"What happened?"" Mother tended to repeat herself until she had a satisfactory answer.

"I fell in the creek." What else could I say?

I could tell from the way my mother sniffed the air that the answer wasn't covering all bases, so I enlarged it. "Trenton went to get me a coat…"

"You fell in the creek? Accidentally? Entirely without help?" Years of parenting, sad to say, had left the woman seriously skeptical.

I nodded, forbearing to speak, hoping I was going to get some of the cocoa. Vala was already raising a cupful to her lips.

"Nobody pushed you? You just fell?"

My mother cast suspicious looks on both Donley and Trenton, never thinking to look in the direction of the real culprit, who was even now the picture of chocolate-smeared innocence.

"I just fell. That's all. I swear it." Swearing impressed Mother. Swearing meant that was the final version of the story, more or less in the fashion of the moving finger having writ, and not one jot ever being capable of change. Not true, necessarily, just final.

"All right," she said. "Go change into something dry. Perhaps you should take a bath first."

I breathed a sigh of relief, echoed in duplicate by Donley and Trenton. But as I entered the hall off the kitchen followed by the other two, I heard Vala say in her most babyish voice, "Momma, don't make me play with Odell and

Donley and Trent again. They called me a bloodhound, and chained me to the kennel."

The three of us stood aghast, out of sight but within hearing, as the loathsome brat poured out the entire story, knowing full well that having sworn, I could never again go back and tell the true version of the Three Billy Goats Gruff and my splash into Moss Creek.

We spent the last two days of our Christmas vacation cleaning out the henhouses, a particularly undesirable task generally undertaken in the summer months when generous quantities of water from the hose took the worst onus from it. It was a toss-up which of us—hens or children—disliked it most. We discussed locking Vala in the henhouse for a weekend next time Mother and Pop went away.

Chapter Six

Carrington was in seventh grade when she asked for piano lessons. “And not from Sister, either.” Sister Seraphica gave lessons for the modest sum of half a dollar weekly, with the added bonus that her students were called out of class to receive their musical education. Carrie refused to say at all why Sister would not do for an instructor, although she was greatly loved and appreciated by her students, especially those who escaped geography.

Mother checked around among her peers and found that private music lessons were available in a number of places, but all at a minimum cost of three dollars at a time. A dollar, Mother had been heard to say, seemed as big as the dining room table, which believe me when fully leafed was large indeed.

“Why not Sister Seraphica?” Mother asked, nearly in despair. Mother had no qualms about our doing without when it meant no bike, wearing the same shoes for school and church, and passing down blouses or sweaters until they had been taken up, let out, dyed, and worn beyond recognition. But piano lessons fell into the category of cultural, mind-developing activities.

"Ragan had voice and the boys play the trombone. I only want to learn to play the piano, not perform," my sister pointed out.

Dragged out of her, that was Carrie's reason for not wanting to take from Sister. Every year, sometimes oftener, Sister put on a musical extravaganza. Paper flowers were glued to cardboard trellises, the nuns' silver candlesticks were dragged out of storage, a new cover was made for the piano bench, and every one of Sister's pupils had, perforce, to demonstrate musically how far they had advanced that year. Admission was a quarter, and the presence of two parents per student was so highly desired as to be considered mandatory. The nuns were business wise.

At twelve, Carrie had no wish to be grouped on the program with the toddlers from first and second grade, who might, in any case be more accomplished than she. Mother could relate to that reasoning; she was as compassionate as the next parent.

Mother accompanied Carrington to the premises of Duncan and Son, Musical Instruments and Training. Mother was intelligent, witty, personable, and gullible. She returned home from that first interview radiant. Mrs. Duncan (Duncan and Son was a family-based firm) insisted that Carrington had latent talent that needed only the guiding hand of a good teacher to be brought to full bloom. Mrs. Duncan was, of course, a professional guiding hand. Carrington would need to have an instrument on which to practice, talent like hers being too profound to wasteand time being of the essence, since Carrie was already twelve years old. Mrs. Duncan was probably surprised at the promptness with which my mother agreed to the need, and no doubt thought it was only a matter of an evening of family discussion before my mother, or better yet, my father, signed for the purchase of a piano and arranged for payments spread over a period of as long as three years. Probably when Mrs. Duncan was remunerated for the first lesson with a crumpled dollar bill, five quarters, seven dimes, and five pennies, she was quickly disabused of that happy notion.

Mother left no stone not only unturned but also completely demolished, in her quest for better things for her children. The next day, carrying a fresh-baked coconut cake with only a few child-sized finger swipes through the thick, fluffy icing, she called on the nuns.

Cannily, she waited until the nuns had brewed a fresh pot of coffee, an unheard of luxury in the middle of the day for women who took seriously their vow of poverty, and cut the cake before she broached the reason for the visit. She was completely candid in her explanation of why Carrie was taking lessons elsewhere. "...and I would never think to ask Sister Seraphica to make an exception to her rule, simply for reasons of vanity..." While they glowed virtuously in the light of the implied compliment, Mother asked point blank for the use of the piano for practice sessions. "After school hours, of course."

It is extremely hard to refuse a favor to a supplicant when your mouth is full of the supplicant's moist, delicious coconut cake. Mother came home with the promise of

Thursday evening and Saturday morning piano privileges. Had that condition prevailed, with none of the rest of us getting involved, things would surely have turned out well. In the fullness of time, Carrington would surely have become a concert pianist, and the world would have lost a great cook.

But after only two practice sessions on the nuns' piano, Carrington was already complaining. Worse than that, she was late coming home. Since it was her job to help with supper preparation, we all suffered.

"It's not my fault. The nuns kept me."

Kept her? Yes, kept. Whenever one of the nuns passed through what they called the music room and spied Carrie apparently aimlessly playing the piano, they thought of some task for her to accomplish.

"Just today, I was sent to the office four times, one time each by Sister Seraphica and Sister Delores and twice by Sister Loretta Louise. And I had to run over to the convent once and help rearrange some shelves in the kitchen for Sister Alphonse. It took me an hour and forty-five minutes to get in my half hour's practice."

"But don't the nuns realize you are practicing?"

Carrie's answer was a shrug. If the nuns realized, they didn't say so. Indeed, Carrie doubted they took seriously any lessons they themselves were not in charge of.

And matters did not improve. When after her third Saturday practice, Carrie arrived at home after three in the afternoon, starved—the nuns had set her to some task while they had lunch, but had not offered her any since she was only going to be there a very short time—Mother decreed that a change must be made.

"I'll just bet the nuns never really wanted me to practice there," Carrie maintained stolidly.

I don't know why it took so long for someone to suggest using Grandmaw's piano. After all, we had all amused ourselves picking out the scales on it every time we went to visit. And Grandmaw seemed pleased with the idea. Best of all, Carrie need not feel herself tied down to any particular time, as Grandmaw was always glad to see her. And perhaps Carrington wouldn't mind, whenever she came, doing a few tasks for Grandmaw, the sort of thing that Grandmaw used to enjoy so much herself but had gotten too old and stiff to do.

"Dust!" said Carrington. "Who gets too old to dust? And shake the throw rugs? And water plants?"

It was simple to see that nobody gets to be a concert pianist without suffering.

The new arrangement went bumpily along for at least a month, and then Grandmaw called. "You know, Jane," she said craftily, "nobody ever uses that piano except Carrington. I haven't played in years. Perhaps it would be as well to move the piano over to your house and then the child can practice every available minute."

Mother at first demurred, thinking it too much to ask of a grandmaw, but accepted with gratitude when Grandmaw assured her that she should think nothing of it. We, misguided bumpkins, all thought Grandmaw was exceedingly generous. So off we went, over the rivers and through the woods, to Grandmother's. There was a considerable contingent of us: Pop and Mom, Carter and Conner to lift and carry, Carrington as grateful beneficiary, Donley to watch, and me because I went everywhere Donley went.

Pianos are heavy. Also unwieldy, inflexible, and awkward. This particular piano had the added disadvantage of having been in the same spot for upwards of a quarter century and showed a distinct disinclination to being moved. First Pop tried to help Conner and Carter, then my help and Donley's was called for, and last the artiste herself was invited to give a hand—and a shoulder. We felt it move—an inch, two inches, a foot. We stood up and rubbed our hands and surveyed the situation.

Obviously, the carpet beneath was the prime source of our trouble. It would be easy enough to move that vessel of arpeggios if we had to contend only with the comparatively frictionless bare floor. So Conner found a tack hammer and freed the carpet along one entire edge. That way the carpet could be rolled right up to the piano, and with a little greater effort, we could lift the piano onto the bare floor and heigh-ho away. It was a really stupid plan.

In the first place, the carpet, when rolled to the edge of the piano, formed an insurmountable barrier over which it would have taken half a dozen of Hannibal's elephants to lift the piano. After the first place, no second place was necessary.

So Conner developed his plan a little further along the same lines. He simply loosened the carpet all around the room. That way, instead of dragging the piano across the carpet, we would drag carpet and all to the truck, and using a bouncing bedsheet effect, simply bounce the piano into the truck. Grandmaw looked awfully dubious but remembered in time that this whole fiasco had been initiated at her insistence. They don't make carpets like that any more.

We dragged and shoved in turn, remembering fortunately to move the rest of Grandmaw's furniture off the flying carpet. "Sprong" said the piano in protest, but eventually, with only a few incidents of smashed fingers, we had that piano all the way across the room where only the newel post, a varnished, highly polished affair supporting a nearly naked female discreetly covered with grapes and such, blocked its way out the front door. Carter was to get in front and guide; Conner was directed to get in back and, aided by us three girls, push with might and main. We did. With all the energy we could muster, Conner, Carrington, Donley, and I pushed until we forced that piano right past the newel post, the passing marked by a crunching sound that boded ill either for the front of the piano or the post. From our places in the rear, we could not discern which until we saw the scantily clad madam fall to the floor, scattering plaster of Paris leaves across the now bare wood of the floor. The gasp I heard was probably my grandmother, since I am pretty sure plaster statues are incapable of the grief I could hear in that one short syllable. Besides, I could see, peering over the keyboard, that the plaster lady had lost her head.

With the obstacle of the newel post removed, it was a cinch to push the piano out on the porch and across to where the truck was backed up to receive it.

The weight of the instrument caused the truck to sink rather low on its axles, and Pop stood inspecting it from every angle before deciding that it would be folly to put more weight on the vehicle, so we children must walk home. After we put Grandmaw's house back in order.

I don't know who is responsible for the fictional grandmother heroine of song and story who loves and spoils her grandchildren, but whoever it was could not have ever come in contact with our Grandmaw, the tyrannical opportunist. She had us tidying messes that had nothing to do with the piano removal. It took us the better part of the afternoon and included the lunch dishes. While the boys hung the carpet over the clothesline ("As long as you have it up anyway") and beat it with a device our Grandmaw assured us had been used frequently in her youth—I had never seen an old-fashioned carpet beater and still have no idea how Grandmaw was able to put her hand on one at a moment's notice—we girls swept and dusted. The plaster lady had made quite a widespread dust, but nothing to compare with the years' accumulation that removing the carpet had uncovered. Finally, we had each item of heavy furniture back in the exact spot it had stood for a generation or two. We knew it was the exact spot because of the indentations on the rug.

"Goodbye, Grandmaw," we caroled cheerily, but Grandmaw was too quick for us.

"We'll have to do something about that big empty spot," she said, as if she hadn't heard our farewells. "There, where the piano was." And sure enough, there was an empty space big enough to hold a square dance. "We'll just rearrange this furniture."

We pushed and pulled. We struggled and strove. We moved each piece of that heavy, solid furniture no less than twice and some pieces as many as four times. I began to wonder about Quasimodo, the hunchback of Notre Dame. Had he once been an ordinary, upright youngster, much like myself, with a grandmother who liked to rearrange her furniture? My eighth birthday was not all that far off, but I was prepared to abandon my "wish list" to get away from Grandmaw's in one piece.

Finally we had the living room furniture aligned to Grandmaw's grudging approval.

"I wonder if you wouldn't want to help me dig up the dahlia and canna bulbs for the winter," Grandmaw said, but this time we pretended we hadn't heard her. I prayed all the way home that they would have the piano unloaded when we got there. God must have heard me, because there it sat, visible from the last turn in the road on the side porch.

"And that's all the further it's going," my father said at supper that evening. "Carrie can wrap a tarp around it when she's not playing it, and next month maybe I'll have time to enclose that porch."

And he did, though rather primitively. Mother was delighted to have both a piano—a real, tangible symbol of culture—and a music room. Pop knew rudimentary carpentry and the side porch already boasted an overhead light, but he knew nothing of sheet metal work, so no heat went out to the "music room." As brisk autumn turned to icy winter, Carrie would open the doors to the kitchen and the dining room, hoping some warm air would flow in the direction of the porch to keep her toes on the loud pedal from freezing and dropping off. Certainly, plenty of cold air flowed the opposite direction, and we complained loudly.

In the very first week of being piano owners, I knew why Grandmaw had been so insistent. Carrie was terrible! Not just poor; not just lacking in talent. Carrie brought to that piano new dimensions in dreadfulness. She never played pianissimo, always fortissimo, and the sound could be heard as far as the barn. I always thought that it was in an effort to contain the sound that my father rushed to enclose the side porch, for the job was begun and completed well ahead of schedule. But if Mother heard the discordance that was a combination of Carrie's playing and the old piano's death throes, she never said so. She beamed encouragement on Carrie as she pounded away and said nothing about the house doors being left open.

After a month of our ears being assaulted by no less than forty-five minutes a day of practice, Mother came up with what she liked to think was a money-conserving idea. Since she was spending three dollars a week on one child's piano lessons and she had six younger children and a piano, what could be more fitting, more economical, than Carrie passing on the benefit of her tuition to the younger ones while becoming more familiar with the music herself? And so four of us became guinea pigs for culture. Vala and Martin were excused by reason of their tender age. Who would force pre-school children out on an unheated side porch to be tortured with amateur music lessons and not have the Children's Protective League on their necks?

Chapter Six

First Carrie would pound out, and I do mean pound out, the tune (and I don't necessarily mean tune), singing along to make it more easily recognizable:

My Grandmaw's house
Is full of toys.
The dolls for girls
And tops for boys.

And we were expected to emulate her. First Luke, then Trent, then Donley and me. Unfortunately or otherwise, we never got to my turn because by then poor Carrington was in tears.

The boys would take their place on the bench, finger the keys, and bawl out:

My Grandmaw's house
Is full of spit.
Be careful or
You'll step in it.

They didn't always say "spit" either.

Finally my mother intervened in sympathy for Carrie and forced the boys to sing the correct words, or most of the correct words, because they then amused themselves by substituting the word "balls" for "tops." Poor Carrie, growing up in an age where girls were tenderly nurtured and sheltered from coarser language, never understood why they laughed so inordinately.

Trent and Luke hated taking the pseudo-lessons nearly as much as Carrie hated administering them, but Mother insisted, even when the boys began to sabotage the piano with wads of gum applied to the strings. Once they went so far as to nail shut the flap that covered the keyboard.

Mother handed Luke the claw hammer wordlessly, and he removed the nails, though not quite as joyously as he had hammered them in. Every night the lessons went on.

Deliverance came from an unforeseen quarter. Carrie had been going weekly to Duncan and Son for over a year when Mother decided to accompany her to see how much progress Mrs. Duncan felt Carrie was making. Tone-deaf—she must have been tone-deaf—Mother sat through the three-quarters of an hour and at the end, proffering her three crumpled dollars, she asked Mrs. Duncan how she felt things were.

"Mrs. Moss," Mrs. Duncan whispered, in respect no doubt, for the savagely assailed ears of all in the vicinity, "You know, no student can make satisfactory progress until they have unlimited access to an instrument." She swept an arm around to indicate to Mother the many models of instruments available in that very showroom.

"But we have a piano."

"You have a piano?" The ice in Mrs. Duncan's voice left no reason to believe that this bit of information pleased her. "You have gone somewhere else to acquire a piano?" This last question was asked in a voice raised several degrees above a whisper.

"Well, yes..." Mother was confused. At first, Mrs. Duncan had made it sound like a piano was a good thing to have, but certainly her present tone was not congratulatory. Mother didn't understand what Mrs. Duncan meant. Later, of course, we realized that Mrs. Duncan was unfamiliar with the family's tradition of trading and exchanging, of handing down and passing up. She must have thought we had gone out and, for heaven's sake, bought a piano, and the idea of a potential buyer going elsewhere for this major purchase must have enraged her.

"Well, you wasted your money. Your daughter has absolutely no talent. Or ability either." The business relationship of one year's standing was thus culminated.

So the piano stood, abandoned, except for an occasional game of hide and seek when some hider would squeeze into the recess behind it. One day, Vala pulled herself up onto the bench and spread her chubby fingers across the keyboard and began to hum to herself in accompaniment to the noise she could make by pressing down on the keys.

"Why, I believe she has talent," Mother said. "I wonder if I ought to arrange for music lessons?" The rest of us went to check the medicine chest for cotton for our ears.

Chapter Seven

I stood very still on the stairs. From here I could hear the voices from the kitchen, which augured poorly for the enjoyment of Saturday breakfast. Too bad, because I knew Mother would have augmented the daily eggs—I think she misunderstood that part in the Lord's Prayer about daily bread—with hot biscuits and, with the first frost a week past, would have allowed us to open a jar of strawberry jam. Mother put up preserves and canned goods for winter, and she darned well insisted that we wait for winter to come before we broke them out.

I knew what the word battle was about because it had been going on all week. One of the customers along Luke's paper route gave him tickets to the circus, and he was counting on going today and told Trent, Donley, and me that we could all go, too. Then last Tuesday, Pop caught Luke smoking an illicit cigarette and grounded him. He also insisted that Luke return all four tickets to the lady who gave them to him.

Luke was as upset about returning the four tickets as he was about missing the circus, and I, too, thought our father was unduly harsh. I hadn't been smoking nor had Donley, and Trent had not been caught. Also, the old lady handed over the tickets only when she found her grandchildren were not able to come for an expected visit and had no use for them anyway. But I had given up trying to understand my pop.

He was leaving the house now, announcing that there was a field of corn to disc up and chores for Luke to do too, and if not, Pop could find something to keep my brother busy. I could hear Luke give the kitchen chair a hard kick, bouncing it against the stove or the sink because there was a tinny clatter.

Mother spoke sharply to him, telling him to control his temper before she gave him a sharp kick. Now does that make any sense? Sure, there were lots of additional marks and scars on the furniture to evidence that they had been the object of Luke's loss of equilibrium, but I thought it better to kick things than people. Now Vala, when she kicked, there was no sharp clatter, since flesh doesn't resound like stoves or cupboards. I had been Vala's choice of kicking often enough to think that it wasn't all that bad to kick a chair.

I sidled into the kitchen, trying to look as if I had been there all along, and the maneuver must have worked because my mother forgot to dish me up a helping of the scrambled eggs from the iron skillet on the stove. I like eggs in their place—everybody knows their place is in cakes and cookies—and I believe in encouraging the hens if they are doing a good job, but eggs every morning?

Looking as unhungry as I could manage, I slid—a definitely different move from sidling—past the kitchen table, managing to pocket four biscuits for private consumption, and announced virtuously that I would go feed the chickens. My virtue went unrewarded because my mother hotly demanded why I was just now getting around to it. The chickens, she announced, should have been fed an hour or more ago. In the interests of keeping the peace and my own health, I did not say that it behooved a mother to be at least as aware of her children's mealtimes as her chickens'. The earlier altercation about the circus had already skimmed off the largest share of my mother's daily allotment of patience.

I hated the chickens. Oh sure, I've heard lots of people say that they just love chicken. They mean liberally coated with flour and egg batter and deep-fried. A lot of folks who just love chicken wouldn't even recognize chicken if the white meat were joined with the dark meat on the hoof, so to speak. Feathered and strutting around scratching in the straw that covered their house floor, crowing over another newly laid egg, a chicken in the flesh is a horse of another color entirely.

I kicked the door a couple of times to announce that I was coming. I had no wish to allow half a dozen to escape the confines of their mesh-surrounded working area and force me to spend half the day rounding them up. Opening the door only as far as necessary to allow entry to my own sturdy self and buckets of chicken mash, I squeezed in, blinking my eyes to adjust to the relative darkness after the bright morning outside. It didn't do to go haring around in the hen house with less than perfect sight. Those roosts are built all the way around, high up the wall, and a chicken is the last member of the animal kingdom whose bathroom habits are a good idea to trust.

Now they came clustering around me, tripping me up in their anxiety to check out the contents of the feed buckets. That just goes to show how dumb they are because they got the same stuff at every meal.

I learned some prize language from Trenton, who was two years ahead of me in school, and the henhouse full of cluckings and scratchings was a perfect spot to try some of it out. During my practices, I managed to get the greater part of the mash into the feeding trays and reached out to pull the hose through the door in order to fill their drinking devices. Just as I was pulling the buckets out the door, one determined pullet squeezed under my arm and into freedom.

I wished I'd gotten a BB gun for Christmas. Then I'd have shot her down in her tracks and no one the wiser. When you have three hundred chickens, one looks much like the other, and they are exceedingly difficult to count. But I didn't have a gun, so I followed the chicken, trying for a nonchalant air as it moseyed along, its head bobbing back and forth, into the barn. Puck-puck-puck-puck. Puck-puck-puck, it said, as it entered. It must have found a hiding place in the dim atmosphere, because I couldn't see or hear it anywhere.

What I heard instead was the voice I recently heard upbraiding my uncaring father for not relenting about the matter of the circus tickets. Luke was saying, in an altogether different tone: "Oh, good boy. Good boy. And aren't you a fine-looking fellow for sure." And then, "Who's there?"

"Me. Odell." I tiptoed past the rusty old farm implements my father wanted to get rid of and my mother insisted on keeping for their incipient antique value. There was Luke and with him a pony. I couldn't believe it! I rubbed my eyes twice and still wasn't sure.

He was the prettiest pony I had ever seen, my acquaintance with the equine world being notoriously slight. He poked a velvety nose into my hand and looked disappointed that I had nothing there for him. Just in time I remembered my hidden breakfast and dug the barely warm biscuits out of my pocket. The pony accepted them daintily and crunched them as I patted his silky coat, where brown and white alternated in spotty splendor, so that I could not have said if he were a white-spotted brown horse or a brown-spotted white horse. Both mane and tail were trimmed to an exactness that bespoke loving care. I wondered aloud how he came to be in our barn, and Luke muttered that he had found him standing around and had put him there.

"But where did he come from?" My question, repeated twice more, was ignored by my brother, who had apparently decided that heavenly providence, as advertised, had provided and his was not to question the way of the Lord.

"Pop will never let you keep him." I didn't intend it to sound mean but Luke scowled. The pony began to lick at my coat sleeve, where some of the chicken mash had slopped, and I thought he must be really hungry to taste that. I mean, that stuff is awful.

"Pop will never let you keep him," I repeated, this time musingly, for even I could see that anything that made such short work of my biscuits was going to take a lot of feeding, and our pop had said more than once that he had all the mouths he could afford to feed and the new litter of kittens would have to go. This particular mouth would literally eat us out of house and home, I thought, as I saw him reach out to taste one of the floor-to-roof supports of the old barn.

"I'm not going to tell Pop." Luke sounded much more confident than he could possibly feel. "I'll just sneak food out to him and keep him hidden."

"Hidden? A pony?" The enormity of what he was contemplating awed me to near silence.

"Well, we kept Conner's pup hidden that time."

Of course we had. A year ago Christmas, Conner had declared life no longer desirable if he had to live without a young hunting dog. And by asking around, Mother had managed to acquire one of not quite impeccable background but reputed to be at least ninety-nine parts beagle hound. For the week before Christmas, the pup had been hidden in a large closet off the bedroom shared by Luke, Trent, and Martin. Whenever the dog had whimpered loudly enough to be heard, Trenton would chime in with his dog imitations and take credit for his natural-sounding rendition of a lonely pup.

The poor pup had a harrowing week of being lowered out of second story windows, whisked out side doors, and shoved under furniture, all so Conner might be surprised

Christmas morning. And we had succeeded somehow, aided by luck and abetted by Conner's willingness to be fooled. And I wasn't sure Pop liked being surprised as much as Conner did. Far be it from me to discourage Luke if he thought we could keep a pony unbeknownst to half the family.

"Where you gonna hide him?"

The barn was out. Although there was plenty of room, our large livestock being reduced to three cows and the shadowy reaches of the barn being adequate for a dozen more, still Pop was in and out of the barn ten or fifteen times a day. Though he himself never undertook the milking chore, he knew how many four-footed beasts were quartered. cows being considerably easier to count than chickens.

"I'm going to take him down and tie him in the willows. That way he can drink from the creek, and we'll just have to carry food down to him."

Luke had worked out in his mind a plan for getting food with no one being the wiser. It involved Martin, my youngest brother, second only to Vala, the youngest when it came to being spoiled. Martin had had a mythical horse living in the bean field since he was able to lisp out the words. Whenever he wanted a graham cracker or some sugar cubes for the horse, he had but to ask. Surely anybody who had for all those years provided marshmallows and candy for an invisible horse wouldn't now stick at a few bales of hay.

We made around a dozen trips back and forth between the willows before lunch. I recruited Donley—I never kept secrets from her—and Luke rounded up Trent to help. And, of course, Martin. We worried about the possibility of Martin's giving away the secret but crossed our fingers and put our faith in luck and our own goodness. We just naturally deserved to have a pony. Surely when God provided one, he could also keep Martin's mouth shut.

Once we were caught with a bale of the cow's fodder, but Martin told Mother it was "for my horse." Trent stood by looking fatuous, and Mother allowed them to carry on. We raided closets—an extremely tricky move—for old blankets and quilts, and rounded up two tired tarpaulins from the barn. Luke intended to construct a tent of sorts for the horse's accommodation. Fortunately, a natural dip in the land hid the willows and the creek from view from the house, and between the site of our furious activity and the plowed fields lay a stand of cherry trees. For now, we were safe.

Using pilfered tools, we strung a line between two large trees and over this laid out the quilts and the tarp. We viewed our efforts with satisfaction. A snug little home with an entire bale of hay and the running water to provide a drink. We didn't give another thought to what we would do when this bale of hay ran out. How often, after all, would Mother allow a little boy's whim to deprive the cows of their fodder?

As I trudged up the hill for lunch, I looked back at the handsome pony and couldn't help thinking he looked strange in his makeshift surroundings. He gave the impression, somehow, that he was used to better things than this.

Marty did prattle at the table about the pony, but everyone had been listening to Marty on the subject of horse/pony for years, so no one even noticed that the color of his steed had changed from shiny licorice black to milky white and chocolate. Martin's mind ran fairly consistently on food. Mother's attention was caught when he remembered once that he had been enjoined to remain mute about matters equine and clapped his hand over his mouth in the middle of a sentence, but then somebody spilled their milk and she forgot.

On Thursday, Luke showed us a further exciting discovery: the pony could do tricks. There was a set of decaying wooden steps leading to the bridge over the stream and the pony could go up and down them with a grace that seemed totally out of horse character. Furthermore, he would occasionally, when ordered, lift his front feet off the ground and standing nearly erect turn in a full circle. I didn't know—maybe all horses could scramble nimbly up and down stairs—but this second thing I knew most ponies could not accomplish. For the first time, I began to think of that pony in conjunction with the recently departed circus.

It rained on Saturday, but nevertheless, my folks set out on their monthly trip to see Grandmother Moss. Mother went, as ever, reluctantly. She had been sewing a skirt for Ragan and was anxious to finish it. She patted the material lovingly as she set it down, the hem pinned in, ready to be hand-sewn.

"I've never spent so much for material," she mused, "but it looked so lovely. Ragan will look so nice in it. But," she cast a meaningful look at Ragan, "if you try to put the hem in it yourself, be careful about letting it trail on the floor. This material can't be washed."

Lucky for us, none of us was expected to accompany our parents on the hour-long drive. Grandmother Moss disapproved of us on the grounds of our Catholicism, which should give you some idea of Grandmother's personality. There were a dozen different reasons to disapprove of us without resorting to religious prejudice.

The car had barely negotiated the turn out of the driveway when we were off to the willows—the five of us—each shouting that he should be the first to ride the pony.

We drew straws, and although Luke tried to cheat, Martin won somehow and sat on the horse while Luke led him up from the shelter of the willows into the still falling drizzle. It was Martin's finest hour. He waved his feet and alternately clapped his hands and clung to the pony's mane. That pony was as patient as any long-suffering animal could be expected to be.

When we reached the tractor path furthest from the house, the path that ran adjacent and parallel with the railroad tracks, Martin obligingly dismounted and Luke vaulted on in a good imitation of the nickel movie cowboys. He rode up and down the path, waving his cap and encouraging himself with loud shouts of "Ride 'em cowboy!" The pony trotted, walked, and cantered as if he too was enjoying the day.

And then the train came. Trains were not all that regular on this particular stretch of track, but indubitably when we were out in the field, the engineer would greet us with a blast of his whistle, a noise we had become so inured to that we hardly noticed. But the pony noticed and that pony had never met a train before. Startled by the pony's abrupt movement, Luke had to throw both arms around the pony's neck in order to maintain some semblance of a seat. The pony lurched sideways, rose on his hind legs and managed to knock poor Martin to the ground. Then he showed us the bottoms of his feet as he plunged headlong down the tractor path, through a gap in the fence, and into Mrs. Klein's back yard.

Mrs. Klein was hanging up or else taking down washing, neither of which looked entirely reasonable in the damp weather. But Mrs. Klein seldom allowed reason to rule her actions. It was a known fact that Mrs. Klein drank; Mrs. Klein drank a lot. Morning and evening, rain and dry: all were pretty much the same to Mrs. Klein. She went through life with a good-natured, booze-inspired smile on her large, freckled face, and while she did not know one of us from the other, she liked us all indiscriminately.

The pony swerved neither right nor left, but met the line of washing squarely, dragging a sheet behind him. Poor Luke. Had he not been crouched over the horse's neck, he would have been decapitated.

In the course of his wild ride, it was borne in upon Luke that even though you ride without a saddle, reins are definitely a good idea. They are sort of like the steering wheel on the car. This pony was entirely out of control, and Luke was helpless to indicate his own wishes.

Only a high fence stopped the pony, and we who were in pursuit saw him come thundering back toward us. Poor Mrs. Klein remained as she had been on our first pass, a clothespin in one hand and confusion on her face. She came unfrozen long enough to reach out and grab the trailing sheet. She still did not quite know what was going on, but as the pony went by she called out cheerfully to Luke, "Don't worry, Conner. I can re-wash the sheets. They weren't dry yet anyway." She waved at the whole crowd as if cheering us on in our new game. She liked kids, she often said, with a bit of spirit.

This time the pony veered off at an angle, and though he was slowing enough for us to maintain—almost—our distance from him, he was still choosing his own way, and that way led, unfortunately, across the area where the hot beds were laid out every year. The hot beds were squared-off, wood-constructed areas where seeds were set out in the spring to raise the tomato plants, cabbage, and sweet potatoes until they were hardy enough to be transplanted in the field. Every bed had a glass cover that was now protected by a covering of boards. It wasn't enough protection. As the pony ran heedlessly on, to our ears came the tinkle of glass breaking and falling beneath the boards. Though the boards were stout enough to bear the weight of the pony, they bowed just enough to cause the glass to shatter. I don't think that pony missed a single frame of hot beds. I heard Trenton trip and fall and mutter a few forbidden words as he came along in hot pursuit.

Now at least we were approaching the barn, and the pony was winded enough that Luke, still clinging tenaciously to his neck, was able to pull himself upright and into a sitting position, giving the impression of being in charge. It was certainly unfortunate that Ragan, apparently disturbed while trying on the new skirt, chose that moment to come running out to the barn to see what the clatter and noise was about. It was even more of a shame that her sudden appearance between the pony and the barn startled the flagging animal anew, and he rose again on his rear legs to execute, gracelessly this time, the circle which had so impressed us earlier.

Poor Ragan drew back in surprise, tripped over a bucket left lying around and fell forwards and sideways into a puddle composed of mud or something worse. Most regrettable of all, I laughed. Later, of course, I remembered what Mother had said about the cost of the new material and that the skirt would have to be dry-cleaned. But for that moment, the sight of my ladylike older sister, who often referred to her younger sisters and brothers as messy creatures, measuring her length in the barnyard was more than I could handle. I paid for it later, of course.

When I had control of myself, I looked around: at Martin, who was cradling one arm in the other, recalling his fall at the start of this wild chase; at Trent, who had fallen more recently and more dramatically on the broken glass from the hot beds and was now bleeding from a cut on the chin and lacerations on both hands; and, of course, at Ragan, who was lifting herself off the ground, a look in her eye which boded ill for all. I thought of the hot beds and shivered. I didn't think we could keep the pony a secret anymore.

Apparently Luke agreed with my conjecture, but he thought faster than I did.

"Hey, Ragan! Just look at the pony we found out here in the yard. I kind of think somebody must have turned him loose on the other side of the hot beds 'cause I heard him before I saw him. We better check for damage over there and then we better call somebody—the police?—and report a found pony."

It took the squad car less than half an hour to arrive, pretty good time considering how far out we lived and the fact that the police driver had apparently stopped to pick up a passenger. The policeman got out of the car first and held the door open for this second party: a short, heavy man wearing a too-tight plaid mackinaw and smoking a skinny little cigar, almost like a cigarette which has gone bad.

"That's him! That's my pony!" He approached and without a word or greeting or even a nod for any of us, began to run his hands across the pony's back, neck, and down his legs. "Where in the devil can he have been for the last week?"

We five who knew exactly where the pony had been for seven days quaked in our muddy shoes but remained judiciously mute.

"Listen, just lemme use your phone. I can have a horse trailer here in twenty minutes," the man said and looked expectantly toward Ragan, now freshly washed and re-attired in her regular Saturday attire of denims. Ragan led him to the house.

"You know," the policeman's voice was soft, so soft it frightened me. "This is a very valuable and talented animal. The circus is offering a reward." There was a universal brightening of our attitudes. "Five Hundred Dollars. No Questions Asked." His tone capitalized every word.

It was a good thing that there were to be no questions, and better still, the man from the circus and the man from the police loaded up our pet-of-the-week and left without inspecting the premises. The blood in my veins ran icy cold as I wondered if policemen, like Superman, are gifted with the vision to see over slopes in the ground, down to the creek where a makeshift stable flapped in the wind.

Marty's arm was merely sprained, not broken, and the doctor charged twenty dollars for putting it in a sling and threw in three stitches for Trent's chin. Mrs. Klein never mentioned to either of my parents or anyone else that she had seen all of us, afoot or astride, that Saturday morning. Perhaps she didn't remember, or perhaps she did remember and wasn't sure if the vision had been hallucinatory. Pop used some pretty strong language when he discovered the hot bed glass, although over half of the glass was unbroken despite my worries. We children never saw one penny of that reward money.

Chapter Eight

Every year at canning season, the barn came into its own. A huge structure, it had been built to house any number of cows, as well as several teams of horses, their equipage, and fodder, and the buggies that had been the means of transportation favored by my grandparents. The last horse died when I was a preschooler, and none of us had grieved for him. A mean-natured beast at best, he had become half-vicious when he was retired in favor of the tractor. Boredom probably accounted for the change, although I could see no surcease of boredom from plodding up and down the furrows of the fields pulling the plow. I thought he should have been happy to have that job behind him.

The three cows who now called the barn home were housed in the far corner in a low, roofed area and were turned out for most of the summer to graze, except at milking time. The whole center of the barn remained empty until we moved in with the paraphernalia of the canning operation. The beauty of using the barn was that little clean up was needed on a day-to-day basis, the dirt floor accepting and absorbing most spills. Of course, as Mom warned us each time we began, anything that spilled, as opposed to dropped, must be left spilled. No attempt to save tomato juice, cooked peaches, or shelled peas must be made. On the other hand, green beans accidentally turned out of the basket were to be picked up and washed. Unpeeled peaches must be salvaged when dropped. The rules were strict and strictly enforced.

Canning time took on the appearance of party time when Aunt Petty and the cousins joined us, as they usually did. In fact, it was Aunt Petty who always knew where a bargain in overripe peaches was to be had and who was selling plums—or even giving them away—to anyone that would pick them. She was also the instigator of trying new things.

"Why not try watermelon pickles, Jane?" she said, "You can't know how well it will work out until you try."

The watermelon pickles were a big success. But the bananas didn't work out so well. Aunt Petty was given three bushels of fruit by the wholesale house one day and offered to share her bounty with us. Even with a total of twenty kids, three bushels of overripe bananas is more than you can use. Aunt Petty thought it would be a good idea to make banana butter. Well, of course, we had never heard of banana butter. Aunt Petty had just made it up. She pointed out that if butter could be made from apples, why not bananas? We remembered with little difficulty how good apple butter tasted and fell to with a will, peeling the remaining two and three quarters bushels of very soft fruit. Bananas have the distinct advantage of being extremely easy to peel. We were finished in record time and the fruit was set to boil with a little water and sugar in the apple butter kettle. It was a desecration of the old iron kettle. Believe me, even a chimpanzee would have turned up his nose at banana butter. It was the first and only time I ever remembered Mother and Aunt Petty actually throwing away food.

Donley and I and the two cousins most near our ages, Sarah and Elizabeth, were set one day to squeezing tomatoes for juice. At first it was fun. We were each given one medium-sized pan, one huge colander, and one mammoth pan to set beneath the colander.

There was a veritable mountain of tomatoes, and Ragan was in charge of the operation. As I grew older, it seemed oftener and oftener that Ragan did less and less and was "in charge" more and more. Her sole duty, and it looked pretty easy to me, was to scald the tomatoes by sinking a wire net into water kept boiling on the stove. Six tomatoes were placed in the container, and it was submerged for the period of time that could be measured by saying a "pious Hail Mary." Often I heard Mother chide someone over the canning process for saying his or her prayers without solemnity and thereby impeding the progress. It took an Our Father to scald peaches in a similar manner. Either they were tougher than tomatoes or they responded better to a plea to the heavenly father rather than the heavenly mother. If one had nothing else to do while the green beans remained in their jars in the pressure cooker, it took two decades of the rosary after a head of steam was gathered for them to be done. And so on.

When the tomatoes were dumped into the smaller of our pans, they were supposed to be scalded to the point where their skins slid off with just a touch of a hand. We took our knives, invariably dull so that we all managed to retain all our fingers, and lopped off the tops of the fruit, quartered it, and plopped it with its five companions into the colander. And then we squeezed. I wouldn't be at all surprised to learn that the isometric exercises so popular three decades later had their origins with a bunch of youngsters squeezing tomato juice for canning.

After a number of times repeating this exercise, we emptied our large containers into even larger containers for boiling and bottling. By that time, our hands were covered with dots the size of the holes in the colanders from the pressure we used on those tomatoes. We were not allowed to throw away any of the chaff from this operation without express permission, since Mother believed that so long as red color could be ascertained, there remained a drop or two of moisture. So we just added more tomatoes on top of the old until the seeds, as well as the solid part of the tomato, were liquefied. Mother could give lessons in persistence to a food processor.

"Are you tired? Is the squeezing wearing you out?" we were asked solicitously when we whined and complained, as we predictably did, when they brought in another bushel of the damned tomatoes. And yes, we would reply, expecting sympathy, since we never seemed to learn from year to year that there was no sympathy to be had. Yes, we were tired of squeezing. Moreover, our arms hurt from the pressure we were putting on the colander, as well as our legs and even our backs. When we whined, we whined in earnest, leaving no possible discomfort unnamed. And finally Elizabeth or Sarah, or perhaps Donley or I, would add in triumph that even the colanders were beginning to bow alarmingly.

"Well, then," we would hear from Mother, and her tone dripped with unctuousness, "You just come sit right here and rest. Yes, right here alongside this bushel of green beans. And while you're resting, just go ahead and snip the ends off these beans."

It was subversive and should not have been allowed. Then, when our fingers were raw from snipping the damned beans, someone would have pushed our colanders back into shape, emptied our juice, and all rested up, we were allowed to go back to squeezing.

The added attraction to snipping beans was that the bean operation was adjacent to where the jelly-making took place, an area where Mother and Aunt Petty spent much of their time stirring and tasting, and altogether making known their positions as the hierarchy of the preserving world. Over in the tomato corner, the four of us "little girls" sat and whispered our secrets and giggled among ourselves. But while we were resting with the green beans, we sat silent, our ears active, to pick up the stray bits of talk we could hear over the hissing and bubbling of the jam kettles.

It was during the canning season that I first heard about Uncle Freddy and his refusal to do the right thing and give the baby a name. I reflected that Mother was the last person who should find fault with anyone for refusing to give a baby a name—considering that names she had given us—but I mulled over Uncle Freddy's refusal and the words used to describe it, and after a couple of years—a lot of water over the dam, a lot of tomatoes in jars, a lot of apples cooked down to sauce—I understood what had been meant. But by then, I suppose the matter was settled.

This year, as I was resting over the green beans, I was surprised to look up and see Aunt Petty with tears streaming down her face. At first I supposed she had taken a "rest" from the strawberry jam to help peel onions for the ketchup, but I was soon persuaded otherwise when I saw Mother put her arms around her sister and administer comforting pats to her back. Mother was smiling. I dropped my head and sighted on nothing further away than the beans in my lap, thus rendering myself invisible. Nothing in the world will stop an adult in full spate of speech except the sight of a not quite adult, or even not quite adolescent, with their head up, looking interested.

"Of course she's young, but not as young as you were when you married Matt," Mother said, and she chuckled.

"Still," Aunt Petty answered with typical adult logic.

"I know, I know," Mother told her, and I could tell from the look on her face that she was ready to launch on a favorite hobbyhorse. "Our children are not as mature as we were at the same age, since they've been given everything they want."

I wanted to jump up, disregarding my lap full of beans, and remonstrate. Everything we want, huh? How, then, did she account for the fact that at nine years old, I had neither dog nor bike. Or even a pink dress like Alice Jane Dougherty? But I restrained myself in the interest of my continuing need to know.

"But it's not as important when she marries as whom she marries, and this boy, Will Poorman, is somebody you approve of, and he's established."

Will Poorman had the farm in the neighborhood of my Aunt and Uncle's house and had been dating my cousin for over a year. So they were talking about Rebecca. It was Rebecca who was getting married, and Aunt Petty was sad about it for some unknown reason. Heck! If someone had been willing to take bossy Ragan off our hands, I would consider it a reason for rejoicing. And I knew, because Sarah and Liz had told me, that there was literally nothing to choose between Becky and Ragan when it came to ordering people around and criticizing those same perfectly all right people.

However, I was missing some of the talk, and I brought my attention back just in time to hear Mother say, "Not before Christmas?" and my aunt admit, "No, the wedding is to be very early in the new year."

It had been possible to talk Rebecca into waiting, although both she and Will had been eager to have it sooner.

"Well, then," Mother shrugged, as if making light of Aunt Petty's worries. But that wasn't what she intended at all. It just wasn't in Mother's nature to worry about matters six months in the future. Taking care of today was her motto at all times. Furthermore, in six months, eighteen-year-old Rebecca would be eighteen and a half and presumably that much more mature. Perhaps they could take away some of that "everything she ever wanted" my

Mother had been talking about and, if Mother was right, that would help make her more grown up.

Three years later, Carter, at age twenty-three, took to himself a bride and Mother wept because he was "too young." I have since come to realize that everybody is "too young" to marry unless their mother has gone to her eternal reward.

The two sisters worked in silence for some minutes before Mother spoke again. Obviously, in the few minutes she had been completely won over by Rebecca's wish to wed without a word being spoken in favor of it.

"Will it be a big wedding?"

And Aunt Petty sighed and imagined that Becky would want it that way. "She speaks of all her sisters being in the wedding, and that means five bridesmaid's dresses."

I could picture Aunt Petty sitting up late at night, bent over her sewing matching at one of her favorite occupations, and the result would be five dresses, none of which would be exactly like the others, but any one of which any girl would love to wear.

I forgot myself so far as to allow my head to come up. Instantly I was spotted.

"Odell, I think you've rested enough." I cast a telling glance at the heap of beans I had snipped during my rest, but subtlety was wasted on Mother. "Better get back to the tomatoes."

Back in the juice corner, I had thought to have a piece of news to tell, but no, Sarah and Liz had been passing the word along to Donley as matter of factly as if there was a wedding in the family every other Tuesday. Donley responded with an I-thought-as-much air that made me want to shake her, since I hadn't given a single thought to upcoming nuptials, and if she had, she had certainly not confided any suspicions to me. All three were disappointed that I had rested so long so near to our mothers and I had no better piece of information to offer than I did.

By the time canning season neared its end, the wedding plans were going forward so rapidly as to make Aunt Petty's whispered information to my Mother seem ridiculous. Sarah and Liz, though they were our favorite companions, were beginning to earn hostility and enmity from Donley and me with their talk of being in the wedding, describing the dresses they would wear and the little velvet headdresses Becky had chosen for them.

At night in our hot little bedroom with its sloping walls that made it impossible to stand upright within four feet of the wall, Donley and I speculated on the possibility of Carter or Conner marrying soon. Sooner even than Becky so that the two of us could steal a march and, to misuse a cliché, "beat Sarah and Liz to the altar." We were unable to hit upon a totally acceptable candidate for any of our family who might have conceivably reached a marriageable age.

For as long as I can remember, at the end of the canning chores, we had a picnic day with our cousins. We took hot dogs to roast over a campfire, and Aunt Petty baked an awesomely large cake. Aunt Petty was a fractionally better cook than my Mother, but in the cake department she truly excelled. We had beans from a can, all the iced tea we could handle, and spent the day in the sand or the water.

It should be noted that these picnics differed in every respect from those we had with our own immediate family, if such a term can be applied to a group of a dozen. When the family embarked on a picnic—without exception on a Sunday, when every other family I knew was wont to embark likewise—the lunch was packed with greater care: fried chicken, potato salad, jars of pickles, slices of tomato, fresh corn locked into a pressure cooker filled with boiled water, and buttered bread. We would then all climb into the car. As an adult, I have been somewhat a habitue of the circus and have yet to be impressed by the number of clowns who emerge from a small car. We not only managed to enter and emerge from the car but rode in it for what seemed endless miles. Moaning and grousing all the way of course.

"Can we stop here, Pop?" The question was always asked ridiculously early in the day. Heavens! We were scarcely three miles from home. No self-respecting man of my pop's generation picnicked less than ten miles from home. The answer was no.

"Can we stop here?" A much later inquiry, but no, we couldn't stop there either. Probably private property, although highway signs seemed to identify it as a public area.

Not the next proposed stop, either; too close to the road and after all, we had small children in the car who were at the present too debilitated by gnawing appetite to be too venturesome. But nevertheless, safety was paramount. So on we went past green meadows and sandy spots near the lake. None satisfactory. We couldn't always hear the reason they were disapproved because the wind from the opened windows blew my pop's words away, but we understood that no diminishment of speed meant "no."

"Can we stop here, Pop?" Encouraged by Vala's enthusiasm, we all chimed in. "Oh, please can we stop here Pop? There's a wading pool and the swings and there's almost nobody here."

"Not even a rabid dog," said one of my older brothers, who was obviously getting too old to enjoy family outings.

Pop turned and swept the entire back seat with an icy glare, as if our unseemly conduct was a deliberate affront.

"If you can't behave any better than that, the best thing to do would be to go home where you can't display your bad manners in public." And the car would turn back homeward and after another hour's uncomfortable drive, we would sweep into our own driveway.

"This looks a likely place. Can we stop here?" We pleaded from the rear.

The picnic would be unpacked on the kitchen table, where Pop liked to take his meals, and hours late, ravagingly hungry, we would eat voraciously of the cold fried chicken and drink the iced tea and not mention picnic for another six weeks.

With the cousins, we wore our oldest clothes with swimsuits beneath. We stopped at the first likely place and laid out the food and either ate or swam, as our fancy took us. Once we forgot the wieners, and replete with bread and butter, pickles and beans, cake and lemonade, no one even cared. After a day in the sand and the water, we were invited to wash off under a freestanding water tap so as to leave a little sand for the next people who decided to come to the beach. We would return home satisfied that we knew how to picnic.

I don't think any of us ever mentioned to our cousins how our pop's family picnics ended. I often wondered if Uncle Matt hated al fresco dining as much as our own pop.

This year Liz and Sarah informed us with dramatically baited breath that Will Poorman was to join us and we could meet him.

"Meet him?" Donley waxed sarcastic. "Isn't he the same hayseed Becky has been seeing for so long?"

Well, yes, he was, though they objected to the term hayseed. The very same Will who had sat with us and licked the dasher from the ice cream freezer, even though he hadn't taken a turn turning the handle and professed a preference for lemon over strawberry; and who had sat on the porch swing and shouted clues while we played Kick the Can and Heavy, Heavy, Heavy Hangs Over Your Head. I looked at Donley with new eyes—well, the same old eyes—but perhaps newly opened. Donley had a crush on Will Poorman and was a little jealous of Becky. I reserved my envy for my cousins who were going to have dress-up dresses and little velvet muffs.

There was a sense of sadness about that year's picnic. Nobody actually sang about wedding bells breaking up that old gang of ours, but the feeling was there. If Becky, not even the oldest of Aunt Petty's children, could be married, where would it all end? We dug deeper holes in the sand, floated further out into the shimmering expanse of the lake in old inner tubes, and climbed higher up the trees than we ever had with a sense of making the last time the best.

Chapter Eight

Poor Will, Poor Will Poorman, we chanted and thought ourselves unbearably clever, and I'm sure we were at least the unbearable part. He was taut, overly polite, and painfully friendly, as if he thought himself on trial. Donley erected a veil of sarcastic cynicism completely at odds with her usual shyly warm personality to hide from everyone but me, who had already guessed, that she found the prospective cousin-in-law more than acceptable.

Trent spied the young couple making for an area completely enclosed by bushes and climbed a nearby tree overlooking the spot, chucking down a handful of pebbles he had pocketed. Becky and Will thought they were being bombarded by a hostile squirrel until they heard Trenton give in to the sheer humor of the situation and laugh so hard he lost his grip and slid down the tree far faster than he had intended.

In an effort to make up in part for the poor manners of her siblings, Ragan proffered the first hot dog that was ready, and was so eager in her insistence that he accept the honor accorded him that she managed to jab him in the thumb with her roasting fork.

Homeward bound, we agreed that in spite of the breech in our family front, Will was an okay sort. But apparently he found us a little less than okay or maybe he just had more family than any prospective bridegroom can safely be exposed to in one day. Whatever the reason, except for glimpses of his backside as he disappeared across the barn lot as we drove in the driveway, we didn't see Will again until the wedding day. And then it took a number of glasses of Aunt Petty's homemade wine to get him through the rigors of the day.

Chapter Nine

We had another memorable picnic that year. Aunt Petty called one night to say that Sarah and Elizabeth were a serious deterrent to her ever finishing the wedding dresses on time. Would it be possible for them to visit us over the weekend? Of course it was. And for their enjoyment, mother planned a Sunday picnic. My heart sank when I heard it. How in the world were Sarah and Liz going to react toward my pop when he rejected one picnic site after another, out of hand? But no, no, said Mother. There was nothing to worry about. We would go to Starved Rock. The state park had even more picnic tables than the entire city parks combined.

Furthermore, it would be a lovely drive—one hundred and twenty miles. The girls would love it. I had other ideas about how the girls would feel, crushed into the back seat of the car and driven one hundred twenty miles starving. How perfectly appropriate that the state park commemorated the place where an entire tribe of Indians took refuge from their enemies and, when under siege, starved to death. I had serious reservations about a culture that commemorated such an event and place.

On Thursday the car broke down. Nothing to get excited about, as our car frequently broke down. Pop would simply raise the hood and remove everything beneath it. With the aid of a block and tackle, he put all the greasy, look-alike parts on various workbenches until he found the trouble. Then he restored the car's innards and away we would go.

I can remember one occasion when his garage work benches were filled with another project. It was a cold winter, and he actually moved the car motor onto the kitchen table. Oh, he put newspapers down first, of course. And for three nights running, he worked on the motor, and we ate supper from plates in the hand or we perched at the counter, which was too high to be comfortable.

On this occasion, he thought it advisable to soak the carburetor in some cleaning solution, which he did, all through Thursday night. Before he went to work on Friday morning, he took it out of the solution and placed it out of the way to drain so it would be ready to re-install that evening. Unfortunately, it was a hard day on the job, and when he arrived home that evening, he had forgotten the out-of-the-way place he had chosen. It is the nature of out-of-the-way places to be less than obvious, so the hunt was on for the carburetor.

It was not in Pop's makeup to believe that he himself was responsible for this foul-up, so he cast the blame around indiscriminately. It was perfectly obvious to him that one of us had taken his carburetor from the place in plain sight where he had put it and, after having a good time with it, had slung it into the weeds where it couldn't be found. If we knew what was good for us, we would find it posthaste.

I had known since I was a tot that what was good for me was to stay out of Pop's path when he was in this particular mood, so I chose to do my searching in the cellar. I scanned all the shelves of canned goods. Not there. I looked around the heap of old newspapers that were being saved for the next paper drive, but that area also was uncluttered by a carburetor. The fact that I had no idea what a carburetor looked like did not deter my search. At least I knew that everything I saw was not a carburetor.

Beneath a massive arm of the furnace—a cold air return—lay a piece of metal that I thought was some kind of junk, so I ignored it. I wandered around the cellar aimlessly, looking only at the things I recognized, and pretty soon I heard the door at the top of the steps open and Luke came slithering down the steps. The closing door muffled the sounds of my father's vocal expression of impatience.

"Do you know what a carburetor looks like, Luke?" Because it was possible that Luke, like me, was choosing to search the cellar only to escape the tirade that raged now over our heads.

But Luke knew. Luke had seen and touched and identified a carburetor. It's wonderful what they used to teach boys and never expected girls to know until some everyday crisis came along, when we were supposed to know everything. Luke made hand motions, drawing a carburetor in the air, its shape, its size, its general configuration. It looked awfully like the chunk of junk beneath the furnace pipe. I ran over to pick it up.

"Something like this?" I showed Luke my find.

"Exactly like that, Digger. That's it."

I looked at the carburetor, and I looked at Luke. Finding something was almost as bad as not finding something. My pop was equally able to deliver a thump on the head to somebody who couldn't find what he wanted or somebody who should have found it much earlier, lying out in plain sight as it was. But Luke had no such reservations.

"Do you mind, Digger, if I take it to him? Pop's pretty mad at me right now because I used all the rubber bands he used to bunch greens with for my paper route. Maybe if I take him what he's looking for…."

As far as I was concerned, Luke was welcome to the find. I trailed behind him—way behind him—as he mounted the steps, the silly old carburetor in his arms.

"Here it is, Pop." Luke interrupted my father's grousing as he stepped through the cellar door. "It was down under the furnace pipe."

This last was an inspired piece of diplomacy. I saw memory sweep over Pop's face as he realized how the carburetor had come to be under the furnace pipe, an out-of-the-way place. Not for one minute would he have admitted that it was he who had chosen that particular resting place. To admit mistakes was to encourage lack of discipline, and Pop wanted no disrespect running riot in our house. I knew that the rubber bands and any other minor transgressions were forgiven Luke for keeping his mouth shut.

Chapter Nine

Alas, even the insertion of the carburetor back in its designated place in the car had no beneficial effect on the car's performance, and even though he fought the good fight all day Saturday, by evening the car was ahead on points. Pop had three skinned fingers and a cut on his arm but the car still had not budged from its chosen position on the driveway. I supposed the picnic was off. I was wrong.

My family honored the Sabbath within reason. Church was an absolute must and punctuality encouraged at all costs, but if you were late, there was a point to which tardiness was, while not condoned, accepted. After that point, church was an experience to be repeated at the next service. While manual labor was decreed to be avoided, some exceptions could be made. The tomatoes could be picked, if necessary. The same went for all the garden produce. However, you couldn't plow and you couldn't, thank the Lord, hoe. You weren't supposed to sew; poor Aunt Petty, who, if Mother was right, would have to remove all her Sunday stitches with her nose. And you couldn't work on a defective automobile. Although if it had been a tractor, Pop might have taken it under advisement.

So, Pop said, having promised a picnic, he would take us on a picnic—in the truck. Oh no! chorused most of the family. The back seat of the car was one thing, but the bed of a truck was something entirely different. Ragan, for one, simply would not go, nor would Luke. Carter and Conner had sworn off picnics earlier in the year, and because they were "older," they were not forced to go. The mutiny spread until Trent and even Carrington were excused from the trip. That left only Donley and me, who must go since the trip was intended to divert and delight our company: Sarah, Liz, Martin, and Vala. I thought of the huge pile of fried chicken Mother had prepared for this outing and decided it wasn't all that bad that the rest of them were staying home. After eating fried chicken two and three times a week for most of my life, it was still my absolutely favorite meat. Of course, no one had ever acquainted me with prime rib and filet.

Pop had built a structure of two by fours and chicken wire that fitted over the bed of the truck, and he had never seen a camper. Too bad he didn't patent his idea, and we would all have been rich. The idea was to keep any of us from falling out—or jumping. We looked pretty silly sitting within this cage, but not nearly as silly as we felt. With this in place, a few blankets and pillows to sit on, and the picnic lunch, we were ready to go. At the very last minute, Pop threw on a couple of tarps—just in case. The six of us children climbed in the back, Mother and Pop got in the front, and away we went…for about twenty-five miles or half an hour. Then it began to rain. Not the drizzle of a day that can't make up its mind what it wants to do. This day knew. It rained more than I had ever seen it, at least up this close. Pop stopped the truck and Martin and Vala—the pets—got to move up front with Mother and Pop. We four girls stayed in the back while Pop pulled the tarps over the wire contraption and tied them securely to the corner posts.

It may have been nice countryside we were driving through, as Mother advertised, but if so, it was lost on us. We couldn't even see each other in the darkness of our improvised camper. There were no openings in the tarp. At first it was fun, huddling in the truck with the blankets pulled around us, because the rain had cooled the air rushing past us at fifty miles an hour. We crowded together to avoid the rain that found its way under the tarp, but that got old. And we had seen Sarah and Liz often enough during the recent months that we had no news to exchange and entertain with. When we cupped our hands against the rear glass of the truck cab, we could see Vala and Marty bouncing around on the seat, fiddling with the radio—actual contact with the world. Eventually we heard the rain stop, but nobody thought about removing the tarp to allow us to see out. Pop didn't even stop the truck. He just kept driving and driving. After about six hours—estimated only, since even if we had had watches, it was too dark back there to read them—the movement slowed and we deduced that we had reached the park.

Strengthened by desperation, Liz managed to stick two fingers through a miniscule hole in the tarp and make a slit big enough to see through. Putting her eye to the aperture, she announced, "Thank goodness, picnic tables and a fireplace. We must be going to stop to eat."

Poor deluded child! Little did she know. She expressed surprise when the truck drove right past that spot and when the second picnic spot failed to bring us to a stop, but after that she was too polite or too puzzled or perhaps too weak from hunger.

"Do you think we could have just one piece of chicken each to sort of tide us over?"

It was Sarah who asked and I realized that she must have read the situation more accurately than her sister. I thought of that veritable mountain of chicken and couldn't see any reason why not. We drew the picnic basket toward us and fished out blindly in the dark until our fingers closed over what was unmistakably crisply fried chicken. We took one piece each. But there was so much there that it seemed all right if we had a second and, after deliberation, a third. When we started on the fourth, we all agreed that we wouldn't have any for lunch, since we already had eaten our share, but just in case we hadn't eaten all we were entitled to, we had a fifth. After that, we didn't even care that Pop kept circling the state park. The scenery may have been all that Mother said it was, but we couldn't see it, but at least we weren't hungry. I think I even napped for a little while. In any case, it took me completely by surprise when the truck actually stopped.

Could we be back home already? I crept forward on stiff legs and was startled to see greenery and a stream and picnic tables. We were actually going to eat out of doors.

From somewhere near at hand came the smell of hamburgers frying and that best of all smells, onions. We must not have been very far from the park concession stand. We hardly knew how to act as we helped Mother spread a clean sheet over the picnic table and lay out the lunch. Even Pop helped with getting things ready to eat, and we realized that at long last, hunger had gotten the better of him. He must have calculated that he was a good two hours from home and a meal at the kitchen table unless he broke down and approved a picnic spot.

Mother laid out the bread and butter and ripe tomato slices, the corn relish, the potato salad, the chocolate cake, and the chicken…three necks, a back, and many, many bones.

I have seldom seen my Pop so unhappy. He was a carnivorous man. It wasn't that he didn't like vegetables and cake and those other good things that make a picnic so enjoyable. It was just that he liked meat a whole lot better. He had been married to our mother for twenty years and in all that time, he had never been expected to eat a chicken back or neck. He lived in a world of all the best pieces of the available meat, and today he was slumming.

"I already had some chicken, so I guess I won't have any more," I said. Donley, Sarah, and Liz said nothing at all but reached for the corn relish. Pop looked dazed but restrained himself from saying anything in the presence of "company." I sniffed the air appreciatively to hint that if he wanted meat, it was available in the vicinity, but Pop failed to understand what I was trying to convey. In any case, I doubt that he would have availed himself of the opportunity to enjoy what smelled so delicious to me. He never ate anything that was not home cooked, preferably by Mother. He solemnly believed that all purveyors of what is now known as "junk food" flavored their offerings with various selections of botulisms.

He ate the chicken back and gave the other three innocent members of our party one neck each. When we had finished our deviled eggs and other non-fleshy delights, we wondered out loud about exploring the park—perhaps even finding the actual rock after which the park was named—but my father indicated wordlessly that we were to climb back into the truck and we drove all the way home. He didn't say much when we got there either.

Donley and I scuttled up to our bedroom the minute we pulled in to our own property, and we didn't come down until after I felt sure he had left in the morning.

It probably took Donley and me even longer to get over the affair that it took Pop. He never again even took us on an aborted picnic, so he didn't get it out of his mind for a few years.

But it was even more years before Donley and I could laugh over it. I told Donley then and she agreed that it served him right. We hadn't had a bite to eat until after he had rejected the first three places.

"Three strikes and he was out," Donley said and we laughed 'till the tears came. But of course, by then we had husbands to protect us and our own homes to live in.

Chapter Ten

Until I was at least sixteen and a half, I was bothered by dreams about Ape Man.

I'll always remember him, the one in the serials who, without warning or intention, became half ape, half man, and the only way you could tell the transformation was about to take place was the spurt of growth his hair experienced. He was a lot like a hirsute Jekyll and Hyde. He went about the countryside doing dreadful things and then could scarcely remember them on the clean-shaven morrow. He was a regular at the Saturday afternoon movie.

We left for the movie—afoot—as soon as the lunch dishes were done. We never sought the information from the feature section about starting times. We got there when we could, and when the flickering images on the screen began to seem overly familiar, we realized that this was the place where we came in and we left with as little ceremony as we had entered.

For a nickel you got to watch two features, assorted cartoons and previews, and a serial. And if you wanted, you could stay through a second showing, provided you came with adequate cash to ensure frequent trips to the snack bar to avoid starvation. To catch the entire offering and remain through it twice, you would have had to forego both lunch and dinner.

We never spent our entertainment budget on the theatre snack bar. It was well known that their popcorn was the same they had had when the movie theatre opened and their chocolate was white with age. Also overpriced. We waited until we left the dim, cool interior of the movie theatre, Once outside, the bright sun smote our eyes, leaving us momentarily blinded. Back when I was a kid, the sun never failed to shine on Saturday afternoons, unless it was actually snowing. Sometimes it rained on Sunday, but never on Saturday afternoon. By and large, everything was managed better back when I was a kid. We made our way two doors east to the ice cream parlor. Sometimes I wonder if I endured Ape Man and his peers just for a chance at the ice cream parlor. It was spotlessly clean and smelled of vanilla and cream.

It took a good deal of soul searching to decide what flavor to order. We drove a long succession of counter girls into the convent by deliberating long and uneasily over our choice. Two dips cost a dime and there was an unwritten but never disregarded law that no kid could have two dips of the same flavor. Even complementary flavors were discouraged on the same cone.

"Let's see," Trent would say, fingering his dime against the glass, thereby allowing the girl on duty to see that he had adequate bankrolling to support his choice. "I had chocolate last week, so I don't want that...not vanilla. Lemon flake...or did I have that two weeks ago? Strawberry. I'll take one dip of strawberry."

The waitress breathed a sigh of immense relief; the decision now being half completed. Within five minutes the top scoop had been decided on, and she could turn her attention to the next customer. Fortunately, our movie attendance was such that there was never a long line at the ice cream counter, even though every kid I knew was programmed to come into the store immediately after he left the movie. Perhaps if we had ever come in at the beginning of a feature and left at the end, we might have encountered crowds there, but we never did. We hated to leave the cool of the store for the heat of the sun-baked sidewalk. Not that we minded the heat for ourselves; we were used to it. The air conditioning of the store and the theatre did not function so efficiently that the change from one to the other was so great. It was just that the hot sun was hard on our cones, and it was difficult to linger over the taste when you had to lick quickly to keep the drops from spattering uselessly on the sidewalk.

On a relatively cool day, we could make the cones last until we were in sight of the drugstore where once again we entered and, sticky-handed, looked over the selection of comic books while we waited for the counter man to take our orders for a coke-to-go (another nickel). I may be misconstruing his motives, but it seems to me that once he saw our strawberried/chocolated/orange-pineappled hands, he never kept us waiting for long. When we left the drugstore, generally our funds were reduced to a nickel each, and we sipped slowly on the coke as we trotted along, the concrete sidewalks giving way to grassy paths along the roadway. Our last stop was a grocery store where, had our mother not been known and her custom cherished, they probably would not have let us in. If our ice cream decision had been hard, it was only training for the choice we were forced to make now.

With the best part of a mile ahead of us and no more stores between us and home, we had to choose something that lasted. At the same time, it had to be something whose taste pleased, too. I mean, you can make horehound drops last all day, but who'd want to? Lemon drops were an excellent choice to fall back on when the imagination let you down, or even an all-day sucker, a misnomer if I ever heard one. I never knew an all-day sucker last a minute longer than an hour and a half, and that was only because of very judicious licking on the part of the consumer. Licorice Allsorts were tempting, or B-B-bats or Bullseyes. All of the above were considered and chosen or rejected before we paid actual cash, and when we arrived each week, it was as if we had never had this discussion before. Each week was a new week at the penny candy counter. I heard once that when the proprietor finally went to the Big Grocery Store in the Sky, his last words to his nearest and dearest concerned the possibility of ripping out the penny candy counter. I never believed that, though.

Chapter Ten

On a certain Saturday afternoon, Luke, Trent, Donley, and I emerged from the movie, our eyes already squinted against the expected sun, our legs unsure of their ability to bear our weight after the hours of inactivity, only to find, against all the rules, the rain pelting down with such force that raindrops hitting the pavement bounced back to reach under the cuffs of jeans to slide ticklingly back down into the shoe. We dodged into the ice cream parlor. Like damp canines, we stood just inside the door and shook ourselves and stared about at the unfamiliar, underwater appearance of the place. Both employees on duty were standing by the window watching the rainwater wash over the plate glass, their rapt breath clouding the window. They turned from their contemplation of the violent weather only with reluctance and returned to the counter to serve us.

"Who's first?" She asked, just as if she hadn't seen us all come together, even as she had seen us every Saturday of the last six.

"I am!" Trent spoke up importantly. If they could play games, so could we. "I want Lemon Flake and Cinnamon Delight."

Trent must have sat through the entire last feature making up his mind about his ice cream cone to have it on the tip of his tongue so quickly. The waitress served him without even noticing that he didn't give any time at all to deliberation.

"That'll be ten cents," she said extending her hand for the dime Trent held ready, before handing over the cone. Next!" she said.

Trent motioned to the rest of us that he was going out to stand in the doorway of the shop while he waited for us, a protected place recessed two feet from the plate glass front. Donley ordered marshmallow and peppermint, and I had peach and black walnut. Luke just closed his fist around a triple dip of lime sherbet, tutti frutti, and maple pecan when we saw Trent being tugged away from the storefront, apparently by a superior force. Donley and I yelled to Luke, and he quickly handed over his fifteen cents.

Luke was always richer than the rest of us, a matter that time has failed to change. We raced to the entrance just in time to see Trent being pushed unwillingly into a car we didn't recognize. The person pushing him was too wrapped in rain gear to be recognized. We thought he mouthed frantically through the window, but before we could reach the car, it drove off.

"The license number! Get the license number!" Luke yelled at us, but the car bore only a small sign that couldn't be read from a distance, but which we recognized from having seen it on other cars: license applied for. We stood on the sidewalk, ignoring the streaming rain for a minute, nearly forgetting to lick our cones. The torrential rain was harder on them than the hot sun.

Then Luke said, "We'd better get to a telephone right away and call the police. Trent's been kidnapped!" He grabbed my arm, toppling the black walnut off my cone and into the gushing, gurgling gutter—lucky for me I had already eaten the peach. I looked back with real regret to see if my ice cream was salvageable, but with Luke tugging at my arm and Donley already hurrying along to the library where we knew Miss Huffy would let us use the phone, I had to abandon it.

Unfortunately, when we arrived at the library, Miss Huffy was not there and her replacement did not recognize us as regular habitués of the place. Indeed, she looked as if she would refuse us admittance if she could. When Luke requested politely to use the phone, she didn't bother to answer but waved him away.

"But I need to make a call!" Poor Luke was too embarrassed to admit that his own brother had the ill grace to be abducted. Surely if he had, the librarian would have granted us the favor. Wouldn't she?

"There's a public phone two blocks over." Miss Huffy's replacement waved a hand vaguely north. We weren't familiar with anything two whole blocks off our established route. Believe me, when everywhere you go, including Sunday Mass (unless you go parent-accompanied), is done by foot-power, you don't cruise around city blocks to discover what's there.

"This is a public phone," Donley spoke up. "The library is a public place supported by public funds. You are paid with public funds, and the telephone bill is paid by our tax money."

Luke and I both stared dumbfounded at our mild sister, who never, never spoke up to people not related closely by blood.

"Well, it is," Donley cried, impassioned. "We pay taxes." That was news to me. I looked at Luke and he looked at me. Of course, there was a two percent tax on retail merchandise, but you had to spend fifty cents all at once before you paid a penny and I never had and I didn't think Donley had very often, either. "We have every bit as much right to use that phone as she does."

"Young lady, this is a library. You can see the sign. Silence please!" the replacement hissed.

There wasn't time to argue. Heaven alone knew what kind of trouble Trent was in, and there was no time to lose. Luke dragged Donley by the arm this time and sought the public telephone. But even as we let the door close behind us, Donley was shouting, "I'm going to tell Miss Huffy. And if anything happens to Trent, it'll be your fault and Miss Huffy will take care of you." It gave the librarian something to think about, anyway.

We bolted down to the public telephone. Luke reached it before we did, and by the time Donley and I had caught up with him, he had turned to look at us, a helpless anguish filling his eyes.

"There's a hole in my pocket. I don't have a nickel."

Donley had only a dime, and the telephone refused to accept it. I dug deep in my pocket and came up with a nickel. Not that I wouldn't have given anything to save my brother Trent, but this meant I wouldn't be able to buy any penny candy at the grocery. And I had lost my ice cream. My eyes filled with tears, and I like to think they were occasioned by my frantic worry about Trent.

After the call, Luke emerged from the telephone booth and reported, "The police said we are to wait right here."

I looked up at the lowering skies that gave no hint that they intended to allow the deluge to stop. It hardly mattered at this point. I could feel my shirt clinging to my back, and

I imagined that further down I could feel my underpants nearly as damp, the rain having soaked through my worn overalls.

Should we call home, we wondered? Our mother always said to let her know if we were going to be late so she wouldn't worry unnecessarily. I always thought it was lots better to worry unnecessarily than have it turn out that it was necessary all along and didn't do a bit of good. When we turned out our pockets, all we had was Donley's dime and five pennies left from my quarter. We would just have to notify our mother and pop when we had more information. We squished our toes in our shoes to pass the time until the police car arrived.

"My God! You kids look like drowned rats!" The police car drifted to a stop right along the curb, and the door opened wide to allow us to climb in. Immediately, I felt chilled. While we were still being rained on, the water had not felt like this. Now, within the car and out of the rain, I wished with all my heart for a large, dry towel to wrap around me. The non-driving officer turned around and took us in: our hair plastered to our heads, drips running down my braids and off Donley's straightened curls. Even Luke had rain puddling down off his short hair, and all the excess water was settling into the upholstery of the car seat.

"The next guy we pick up better have his rain gear," the cop pronounced and left it at that. "So what's you kids' problem?"

"You mean they didn't tell from headquarters? Our brother's been kidnapped." Luke told the story while Donley and I huddled far into the dusty upholstery of the back seat for warmth.

"And the car had no license plate? What kind of car was it?"

"Yellow," I said.

"Packard," said Luke. They directed their further questions about car and driver to my brother.

After a muttered discussion in the front seat—which was largely devoted to the possibility that we had made the whole story up and the ramifications for themselves if they chose to believe or alternately disbelieve the whole thing—they came to a decision to call in a report and to cruise the neighborhood to see if any of us could sight the car or the boy. We gave them—all at once and then separately—all the details they asked for about Trent's height, weight, color of eyes, and wardrobe of the day.

"And he was carrying a double-dip ice cream cone—cinnamon and lemon," I volunteered, but the police chose either to disbelieve this last or consider it of little importance, as they just laughed and did not include it in their report.

We cruised the neighborhood, the three of us in unwarranted luxury in the back seat, peering out at the passing scene. I forgot for minutes at a time that we were seeking clues as to the whereabouts of my brother who might be suffering murder and dismemberment, even as we searched. Sometimes I wished the cops would go a little faster so that no one would spot our unlikely trio in custody, and other times I wished they would go a little more slowly so that I might see the better into the shop windows we passed. The Western Auto Store had about twenty-five bikes of every color and description, and I would have liked to check them over.

Up and down deserted streets the car swept, the rain drumming on its roof, the water beneath its wheels splashing up against the glass on my side. I think I fell asleep, but only for a little while. I woke momentarily confused and then was struck by conscience, wondering if in my sleep I might have failed to spot some clue, unrecognizable by anybody but me, that would have led us to Trent.

And then a disembodied voice came squawking into the car through the dashboard, "Car Fifty-eight, come in please." Our own officer picked up the microphone, said something cryptic into it, and the voice responded, "We have another report of a kidnapping in the same neighborhood as yours." The two officers looked at each other, taking us seriously for the first time.

"We have three kids missing on their way home from the Weston Street Theatre."

That meant, counting Trent, four kids were gone from the very movie theatre we had been attending. It must have been some large-scale criminal operation. I could see my name—maybe my picture—in the paper, front page.

"Just a minute, Car Fifty-eight. This is interesting. The kids that have gone missing must be relatives of the kid reported kidnapped earlier. The name is Moss here, too."

Did that mean Carrington and Ragan and possibly Conner had been kidnapped? We were the only Moss kids I knew who went to the movie on Saturday afternoon, and believe me, after the Saturday afternoons we had spent there, I knew everybody. If four of us had been made off with, I shuddered to think of poor Mother and her worrying, this time necessarily.

"Maybe you better come in, Car Fifty-eight."

We made a U-turn and headed for the police station.

We were ushered up broken concrete steps, through a hall that needed painting worse than our chicken house and into the police station proper. There was Mother, looking just awful. So they must have had to notify her, and my heart went out to her. And there was Pop, looking more thundery than the skies outside, and there was Uncle Freddy, looking very annoyed. And there was Trent.

"You've found him," we shouted joyfully.

"You've found them," Trent said in chorus with us.

"What the hell is going on here?" said Uncle Freddy, interrupted by Pop asking, "Where have you been and what have you been doing?" Neither his voice nor Uncle Freddy's carried one hint of joy.

The cops conferred with Mother, torn between relief that her large family remained intact and irritation that she had been dragged out on a wet Saturday afternoon. It was clear that she was allowing the relief to wane and the irritation to wax.

"Let's see then," said the officer in charge. "Your brother here picked up your son—one of your sons—from the movie in his new car…"

"You have a new car, Uncle Freddy?" The enthusiasm in Luke's voice at any other time would have been enough to kindle a like emotion from Uncle Freddy, but just now, Uncle Freddy was disinclined to discuss automotive affairs with Luke. Waving a dismissing hand, he let Luke know this wasn't the time or the place, and Luke subsided.

"And your other children, not recognizing the car since it was new, feared that their brother had been kidnapped?" Mother agreed, with a nod of her head, that so far the police had the story straight. "So then," the cop summarized, "We sent Manning and Horst out to pick up the kids, hear their story, and drive them around looking for some sign of the first boy's whereabouts. Then when the kids didn't show up at home when this boy thought they should," he pointed at Trent, "he called us to inform us that the three of them were missing."

The policeman looked around as if to claim credit for telling so succinct a story. I waited for somebody to say that if the police had called home—they had, after all, phones coming out of their ears, I could tell by the continuous ringing sound that penetrated to this outer office—while we had been fresh out of nickels. If they had talked with somebody there, most of what had happened need not have. But nobody did say it. It was like a conspiracy of adults present to shift the entire blame on the four of us. We all stood around looking at each other, a few last drops splashing off me, Donley, and Luke onto the grimy floor, for another minute or so, and then one of the cops said, in a strangled voice, "Well, all's well that ends well."

Little did he know, this matter wasn't ended. We would be hearing about it for weeks.

"You might as well all go home, folks. There's nothing else that I know of."

As we left the big policeman sat down hard on a chair, and I could hear him laughing all the way down the hall. Pop could hear him, too. I could tell by the reddening on the tips of his ears.

Of course, you cannot bring your children up to respect the authority of the police force and then punish them for contacting those same minions of law and order when they think the need arises. But when we got home, Pop found a couple of things that called for discipline. Wisely, Uncle Freddy declined an invitation to come back to the house to complete his interrupted visit.

The lunch dishes had been poorly washed, and Donley and I were to empty all the lunch dishes back out of the cupboard and re-do them. Pop, of course, helped by getting down everything, right down to a funny-shaped glass dish Mom only used to serve cranberries. I knew darned well we hadn't used that for lunch. We hadn't had cranberries since Christmas.

Trent and Luke were sent down to tidy the cellar, a far worse fate that ours. Pop said he told them to tidy up the tool bench last week and they hadn't bothered.

We went down to check on their progress after we had used the last available dishcloth to dry those thousands of dishes.

"Trent," I said, speaking in a whisper. "It sure looked to me like Uncle Freddy was forcing you into that car."

Well, of course, it hadn't looked like Uncle Freddy forcing. Had we recognized our uncle, perhaps we wouldn't have called the police. But Trent knew what I meant.

"He did!" Trent swept a few feet further along the brick-laid floor that hadn't been clean, really clean, since Teddy Roosevelt stormed up San Juan Hill. "I didn't want to go with him and miss out on the drugstore. I had that dollar from Grandmaw for my birthday, and I wanted to buy some comics. I said I'd just walk home, but he insisted that I ride. I was trying to tell you guys to buy me some candy at the grocery, and I'd pay you back when I got home."

Trent seemed so aggrieved that I wanted to tell him about my dip of ice cream abandoned in the rising waters of the gutter along Weston Street and my nickel lost forever in the greedy maw of the telephone, but just then Pop started down the steps. Donley and I thought it the better part of discretion to make our exit out the exterior door.

"Anyway, it was a good movie," she told me as we headed for the barn and the chicken feeding chore. "Especially that second feature...the one about the kid who gets kidnapped."

Chapter Eleven

Every school in town put on an annual play, but whereas the others spent their energy vying for best Christmas pageant, our school gave it a couple more months and saved our time and talent for the great and glorious seventeenth of March. Father O'Hara's decision, doubtlessly. The reasoning behind the selection of dates, other than the obvious one of glorifying heaven's first citizen with a brogue, was that while the other parochial schools had to compete for the Christmas crowd, we alone, St. Albert's, put on a spring performance. Thus, anyone in the mood for a school performance had little recourse but to attend ours, the nuns told us, completely disregarding the fact that nobody attends school performances unless they have someone of their own blood in it, and then they do so only under protest after notifying God of their intentions so that he can be certain to make a record of it and credit their account in the Good Book. Nevertheless, when the other kids were laying away their costumes, wings, halos, and stuffed sheep for next year's performance, we St. Albertians were dusting off our shamrocks, fairy costumes, and practicing our lines.

My biggest role ever in the school play was as understudy to a girl who recited a long, narrative poem about a family who said the rosary every night. I hoped and prayed that she would fall victim to a plague or break a leg. Certainly a simple broken arm would not have kept Kathy off the stage when she had gone to all the trouble of memorizing at least eighty lines of poetry, but alack and alas, her health continued to bloom.

Donley once had a two-line part in a one-act skit, and Carrington always sang in the chorus. My brothers, when coerced or cajoled, agreed to help backstage, mostly because the performance was followed by cake and ice cream for all comers. But in all our family, Ragan alone ever managed a starring role. And then she had to share the stage with Vala.

Naturally, all of us were expected to buy a ticket—buy a ticket? What was the world coming to when the families of the stars had to buy their way into the theatre? I consoled myself with the promise of infinite varieties of cake to come.

By the time we parked the car and made our way into the parish hall and paid our three dollars to cover Mom and Pop, Grandmaw and Grandpaw, and the eight of us not currently active in the world of show business, there was only room enough to seat ourselves together in the very back of the room. We barely had time to settle in before the curtain opened.

Chapter Eleven

Vala was first on stage. At five years of age, she was still short and still wispy of hair. She was dressed now in a mint green costume with a net skirt so full it stuck out and touched the pale yellow of the fairy standing a double arm's length from her. You could tell they were fairies because they sported wings and each carried a magic wand tipped with a star. At first sight of her, Mother drew a hanky from her bag and began to wipe proud tears from her eyes. She didn't notice there were at least twenty other mothers at any given moment in the body of the hall also wiping moisture from their eyes. The chorus line formed itself, with Vala very last in line.

"They always put the best dancers on the end," Mother confided to my father and the four rows immediately in front of us. The chorus line opened their collective mouths to sing about the dell where the little folks live on the misty isle that dropped from heaven. As they started the first chorus, they accompanied their song with a dance number. Shuffle, shuffle, hop, kick, they went to the left, and Vala drew near center stage. Kick, kick, hop, hop, they went to the right, and Vala disappeared from view. They repeated the first set of steps, and Vala re-emerged onstage. Something was very wrong here. The lavender fairy on the left end maintained stage presence literally. It took a moment to realize that the tallest fairy, backed up by the number one leprechaun was a good ten feet right of center stage. Everytime the dancers moved to their right, Vala lost her place. They moved to the right fairly often, as it was a very long dance sequence, designed to get the most from the pretty piece of change each mother paid for the costumes. On the third such maneuver, poor Vala apparently tripped over something in the wings and came back with her dress a little dusty and the skirt partially pulled away at the waist. She had lost her timorous smile and in its place, grim determination was born.

"Look at that Vala!" Carrington's voice was not muffled at all. "They keep pushing her offstage, but she keeps kicking and clawing her way back on."

I tried very hard not to laugh, but next to me, Donley was also trying and failing. Her shoulders shook with mirth. Next to her, Trenton was scrunched down so far in his seat that his elbows were nearly touching the floor. On the other side, Conner and Luke had given up the fight for sobriety, and I surrendered, too. I put my head down so that my father, whose patience and tolerance were so little developed as to be nearly non-existent, could not see that it was I who was making those snuffling, hiccuping noises, but I could still feel the heat of his anger from four seats down. Even Grandmaw was having a difficult time restraining herself, but when Vala returned to the stage after the fourth rightward movement of the chorus line, she guffawed, and further attempts at self-control were useless. Laughter rang out from the entire row with the exception of my Pop, who maintained his frosty, disapproving look, and soon the whole auditorium rang with it. I imagine it was the most successful number of the entire production. When it was finally over, Mother wiped her eyes, but whether tears of laughter or pride, I didn't know. Pop's feelings went unaired, as he hardly spoke to any of us for the rest of the evening.

Then the play itself began. The nuns authored the play, perhaps to allow some outlet for their dramatic ability, perhaps to save the cost of purchasing rights, but infinitely most likely so that the available costumes could be best used. That was partially why Ragan was in the play this year. For all intents and purposes she was not eligible, having graduated from St. Albert's. But when she was a student in the school, no one had realized that she had a Voice. Not a voice—we all knew she had one of those, for we had all heard her ask for the salt to be passed, for more room in the car, and for a cessation of noise. "Shut up, you guys!" Ragan had been saying for years. No, a Voice was used only for singing, reciting, and projecting.

Having passed over her for seven of her eight years while she was among them even as the Old Testament prophets were deemed of little account by those they knew best, the nuns now saw an opportunity and used it. Besides that, Ragan had the costume they needed. She had been in a play at the high school and the St. Albert's nuns, always on the lookout for promising material, had taken note of the costume—Kelly green and gold—and found it not unpleasing with their color scheme.

So now Ragan stood on the stage and told us that she was an Irish colleen who was engaged to a millionaire from America, and as much as she loved this misty isle, she must leave, perhaps forever, to go and live in splendor with her besotted fiancée, having first become his wife. Those nuns did not allow any hint of lasciviousness in the program. She sang a couple of songs depicting these feelings, accompanied by the chorus line (Vala's dress had been hastily mended). Next to me, Donley was becoming as restless as I was myself.

"In two days," Ragan declaimed from the stage, "I must leave all that my heart holds dear and venture into the unknown."

"Hah!" answered Donley. "I knew this play couldn't go on forever. Her ship leaves in two days."

Once again the Moss family had been heard from, and once again the spectators didn't mind a bit, welcoming a little light relief from the intense action of the play.

The minute the curtain descended on the last part of the program, Pop stood up and announced his intention to leave immediately and go directly home. He was greeted with incredulous looks from all eight of his children present and their grandparents.

"What about the cake and coffee?" It was Conner who asked, but he spoke for all of us.

"There's cake and coffee to be had at home." Pop said. Big surprise for him: there was not. The two cakes Mother had baked that day and to which he was probably referring were even now being cut into pieces in the kitchen section of the parish hall, but no one cared to contradict him.

"I don't think it would hurt to stay a little while," Mother said, and I knew she was looking forward to hearing everyone say what a lovely voice Ragan had. Because it didn't matter how boring the play, Ragan had acquitted herself proudly. But Pop was adamant. Anyone who didn't want to come home right now could walk later. Eight voices opted for a moonlit walk; only Grandmaw and Grandpaw, besides Mother, coming down on the side of a ride home now, but then they lived farther away than we did.

Grandmaw pressed her ticket and Grandpaw's into my hand for me and Donley to use.

"I hope you don't mind stopping by McCarthy's, Frank" I heard her say as she trailed reluctantly from the scene of social activity. "Pa and I need to get a gallon of beer if we're not going to have any cake to eat."

He likely did mind, probably a lot, but he would stop anyway. Pop had preached too often to us about honoring parents to not do what Mother's parents had asked him so nicely to do. I hoped, meanly, that Grandpaw would plead arthritis and send Pop in the tavern for the jug of beer. Pop didn't patronize taverns much. They fell well within the scope of what he disapproved of.

With our parents and grandparents departed, we didn't have to be on our absolute best behavior. There are a lot of things that people will complain about if a parent is on the spot that aren't serious enough to make a telephone call over. I found Donley, and we went to look over the cake offerings.

"One piece each, girls!" Mrs. Hannahan was the self-appointed enforcer of rules that she'd adopted single-handedly. There she was, reigning over a table that stretched half the entire length of the hall and totally covered with cakes of such a variety that nobody could expect to narrow a choice to one piece.

No church function could get going without Mrs. Hannahan, or at least she gave the impression that such was the case. She was the kind of person who gave new meaning to officiousness. In her ruffled organdy apron, spotlessly clean when she arrived for her stint of duty and equally clean when she had completed her volunteer hours, she was much better at designating tasks than at undertaking them. My mother said often that she admired Mrs. Hannahan inordinately, in a tone of voice that said she could tell you a thing or two if the children weren't here. She was universally disliked.

I informed her now that I had two tickets—my own and Grandmaw's—and I thought I would have chocolate and that funny colored piece that looked like it might be spice or butterscotch.

"Who's the second piece for, Miss Moss?" Nasty old gorgon. She couldn't possibly remember my first name so had found a way around using it. "I saw your grandmother leave a few minutes ago."

"They're both for me. And Donley gets Grandpaw's piece."

"Sorry," she lied. Anybody could see that she wasn't a bit sorry. "No seconds for greedy little girls." And she slapped my hand when I reached for a second piece in spite of her.

I was indignant. I had two quarter tickets, bought and paid for. I was entitled to two pieces of cake. For goodness sake, each cake was cut into at least twelve pieces and our own mother brought two cakes, which added up to twenty-four pieces, and I wanted at least two. Subtle tactics were called for, so we went in search of help.

The Larkin girls were our best friends. Madonna Larkin was in my grade and Jenny was in Donley's. We worked out a plan that was beautiful in its simplicity. The table was so long that even nosy Mrs. Hannahan couldn't take care of both ends of it. The Larkin girls went to stand at one end of the table and began to point at the cakes. Once Jenny licked her finger after pointing very closely at a dark slice, and Mrs. Hannahan was worried that the girls were actually putting their fingers into the cakes. I thought it wasn't altogether unlikely myself. Donley and I stood together at the other end of the table, and Mrs. Hannahan was torn between preventing us from getting that extra piece of cake and keeping an eye on the icing on the Larkins' end. Finally, the Larkin girls began to lick their fingers each time they pointed, then laughed uproariously. Mrs. Hannahan couldn't stand it anymore. She rushed to their end of the table and immediately Donley and I fulfilled her worst fears and made off with three slices of cake each. After all, our ticket entitled us to cake and coffee, and we weren't having any coffee. The lemon and chocolate were delicious, but the spice cake was a little dry.

In the meantime, Mrs. Hannahan rushed to the opposite end of the table and administered her sharp little slaps to the now dirty fingers of Madonna and Jenny. Pretty soon we would have to get up from our places and try the same scheme in reverse to make sure our friends got what they wanted from the table too.

There were a lot of gaps in the plates of sliced cake when Trenton came out from the back room. He looked a little glassy-eyed, and when he slumped down in the chair beside us he asked us if we were ready to go.

"I must have eaten twelve pieces of cake," he moaned, "and I got my hand hurt when someone accidentally slammed a drawer on it." He held up his right hand to show us the line of red that even now was slightly puffy, the red welt extending across all four fingers. "Play that right, and there'll be no school work for me tomorrow." It was his right hand.

I don't know whose idea it was—perhaps all four of us girls thought of it at once and spoke together. "Trenton, why don't you go get some more cake?"

"Are you crazy? If I ate one more piece of cake, I'd bust wide open."

Once we'd explained our plan to Trent, he embraced it eagerly. He rose and sauntered over tc the table, and rather than stand directly in front of Mrs. Hannahan, he moved down a few paces as if he were trying to avoid her eye on him. The move made Mrs. Hannahan immediately alert, like a dog on the point in quail hunting season.

"Mmmm, let's see," Trenton spoke to himself, as if he were alone in the large room. "I've tried chocolate and co-conut, but what about angel cake?"

"No you don't, young man. One piece of cake to a cus-tomer."

But Trent was obviously deaf to her words. He reached out for the largest piece of angel cake and for his troubles received Mrs. Hannahan's trademark: a quick slap on the hand.

"Oh, ouch, oooh, golly!" Trent's anguish was heard in the furthest corner of the hall. "Omigosh, you've broken my hand."

People were turning to face Trent, and some of his classmates were heading over to see what the trouble was. Trent raised his voice, something I thought physically impossible.

"Whaddaya got in your hand? Whadid you hit me with? I think you've broken my hand."

Now several of the women from the kitchen were coming out, and one of them played right into Trent's hand, so to speak, by asking what happened.

"She hit me. I think she broke my hand." Trent squeezed out a few real tears. "I wasn't doing nothing. I worked in the kitchen all night and didn't have time to eat anything, and now that I come here to use up my ticket—I paid a quarter for it, after all—and now she slugged me." For evidence, he held up the hand with the welt mark. "Look at that. It's swollen up already. I bet I need x-rays. I bet it's broken."

There was one brief moment when I thought everyone would laugh at Trent and shoo him away, but then Mrs. House spoke up.

"Lordyday, Prudence," for such was Mrs. Hannahan's given name and might have accounted for whatever lack of personality she had. "What did you hit the boy with?"

She motioned for someone to bring her the first-aid box and somebody instantly complied. Mrs. House bathed Trent's injured hand with some solution while all the time Trent writhed and grimaced with soundless pain. Mrs. Hannahan writhed equally silently, her face flaming with color, in much more intense pain. Mrs. House wasn't about to let her off, either.

"What was he doing, Prudence, that you hit him so hard?"

Mrs. Hannahan spluttered about Trent's having reached for a piece of cake when she was gospel sure that he had already had several pieces and that she had made a rule that each child could have only one piece.

It was amazing how quiet that gigantic old hall was. There hadn't been such shushing for any performance in the program. Everybody waited to hear what Mrs. House would say. But Mrs. House disappointed them. She just shook her head and said nothing. It was left for Trent's school friends to mutter loudly that perhaps Trent could sue or, at the very least, demand his quarter back since he had been deprived of his rights. Trent remained soulfully quiet, as befitted a martyr to the cause, and allowed pain to play over his features.

"I'm going to have another piece of cake and see if she hits me," one of the boys said. I thought it was Gordy Moffett. And the cry was taken up eagerly. Mrs. Hannahan was utterly routed.

Mrs. House packed up an uncut cake for Trent to carry home, along with instructions about treating his injury, and we prepared to leave. As we went out the door, I looked back and saw Father O'Hara talking to Mrs. Hannahan, his expression suitably solemn, hers apologetic, verging on tearful. I don't think she ever helped out with another church supper, ever.

We ate the cake on the way home. It saved explanations.

Chapter Twelve

When Luke was a toddler, it became apparent that his hair, soft and curly, was not going to darken the way the rest of ours did. Luke's was as yellow as an Easter duckling. Furthermore, it also became apparent early that he would not be as big—measured floor to hair—as his brothers. He walked kind of funny, too. So when somebody said affectionately, "He's just like a little duck: Lucas Joseph Duck," the name adhered tenaciously and not always affectionately.

Luke was the consummate businessman. Probably he set some kind of longevity record with the local paper for number of years employed as a carrier. He began the job at the ripe age of eight, over the violent objections of Mother. She was afraid to have him cross the highway a block from the house on his bike. Unless he crossed the highway, there was nobody to deliver papers to except an alcoholic old lady and the Elstons. He offered to ask if any newspaper customers were willing to get up early in the morning and meet him across the highway so that he could toss them their papers without crossing, but doubted that he would get any volunteers.

Mother gave in and allowed him to acquire a route. Perhaps she thought his humor was a saving grace and the angels would be enchanted enough by it to watch carefully over him as he threaded his way through what traffic existed at six in the morning. Or perhaps she thought that anyone with his sense of humor didn't really deserve to be protected.

In time, Trenton, seeing how much spending money Luke managed to garner with a paper route, also applied for and was granted one. Alas, poor Trent was made of less stern stuff. When Luke was lifting the heavy paper bag onto his handlebars, all newspapers rolled stiffly and secured with a rubber band, poor Trent was still wiping the sleep from his eyes. Often enough, as Luke threw one leg over the frame of the bike and prepared to coast downhill along the drive through the misty dawn, Trent was deciding that ten more minutes in bed never hurt anyone. Somehow, Trent never found a paper route as remunerative as his slightly older brother.

Luke had another decided advantage that not only Trent, but every other paperboy I ever met, lacked. It was a secret weapon: four-legged, long-toothed, longer haired, named in a burst of youthful creativity, Dog. Dog had several disguises, mostly that of a hairy, lumpy throw rug. When curled in a ball, his nose stuck beneath his long, feathery tail, Dog looked totally inanimate, a room decoration of dubious taste, kicked into a pile. More than one visitor had been known to drop a hat, a pocketbook, even a cup of coffee, when, without warning Dog would stretch out all four legs, raise his head, and display a long, friendly pink tongue.

"Look at their eyes," Mother used to tell us about strange dogs. Only by seeking their souls within the depth of their liquid eyes could one know for absolutely certain whether a first-met dog was a biter or merely a barker. That strategy was doomed to failure in the case of Dog. I am perfectly certain that Dog had eyes because now and then I would raise the heavy hanks of hair that hung over them and check. Sooner or later, I always found a matched set. But I never saw them without actually seeking them.

Dog's second disguise was the weapon Luke used so successfully on his paper route. Several customers, probably golden of heart, were pretty mean on the surface. When Luke came to call on Saturday for purposes of "collecting" for the paper, they were wont to greet him with surly words, non-response to his repeated knocks on the door, or actual threats of physical violence. That was before he acquired Dog, the paperboy's friend. When Dog had attained approximately half his rather daunting size, he began to follow Luke wherever he went. Rain or shine, except in stormy weather, cold or sultry, Dog went lolloping after the bike, circling around, and coming back when Luke was unable to pedal as fast as Dog could lollop.

On the first Saturday that Dog went on the collection round, Luke marched fearlessly up to the door of one of his worst offenders and knocked sharply. The gentleman came to the door, looking like less than your average matinee idol. Unshaven, dressed in a tee shirt and a pair of wash pants at odds with the washing machine.

"Sorry, kid, not today," he said and prepared to close the screen door in Luke's face.

"Arghgrr!"

The gentleman looked down (at half size, Dog could still be looked down on) and seeing the dog's legs stiffening and his hair standing up straight on his neck, deemed it advisable to retreat. He closed the door and snapped the screen lock. Feeling safe, he couldn't resist a taunt.

"Might try again tomorrow, kid. You never know when my ship might come home." Dumb guy couldn't even get the cliché right.

Dog flung himself at the door and, rising up on hind legs, ripped the rotting screen wire from eye level to within half a foot of the bottom and prepared to enter uninvited.

"Call off your dog, kid." The paper customer lost all bravado.

"I can't," Luke shrugged helplessly. "He doesn't have a collar and leash, and I can't buy him one until I collect the rest of my paper route."

Money changed hands forthwith, and Luke and Dog went on to the next difficult customer. Lots of them even included a tip, for which favor Luke instructed Dog to remain on the sidewalk but within sight on the next visit.

It was a good thing none of those people ever saw Dog during a thunderstorm. Once you saw that, you lost all awe of him. Dog lost his status as lapdog within six weeks of his birth, yet when the heavens grumbled and flashed fireworks, he headed for the nearest lap and tried to crawl in.

Failing a sympathetic lap, he sought shelter behind the sofa or under or in a bed. It was better all around if he avoided both Pop's and Ragan's. Both of them reacted badly to the discovery of black dog hairs on their sheets. If some ill chance allowed him to be out of doors when a thunderstorm hit, the air was rent with piteous howls and hysterical barking that could move the stoniest heart. Dog earned himself a place in our family annals second only to Betsy, the hunting dog of renown and fame.

After Dog became a part of his life, Luke's fortunes waxed, and while the rest of us sat around listening to Jack Armstrong, the All American Boy, and Sky King and wished we had the money to send for secret decoder rings and be the first in our neighborhood to own a genuine sheriff's badge and whistle, Luke charted his financial ambitions.

So that even as I prayed nightly for a bike of my own or a zippered notebook (I eventually got the latter for Christmas but have lived out the years of my life to date without ever acquiring the former), Luke counted the money he had and how much more he needed to achieve whatever was catching his fancy any given week. Never a bike; he already had one. It had belonged previously to Carter and before that to one of the Donbeam kids across the highway. A bike, nevertheless. And if it won no prizes for beauty, it was kept running well by a weekly tune up.

One spring day Luke knew that he had to have—not just wanted but had to have—a Daisy BB gun. For the last two Christmases, he had asked for one in a desultory way, knowing full well that what he would get was warm socks and perhaps a new football, with the warning that BB guns were notorious for causing grievous bodily harm.

So, of course, he said nothing to anyone but Trenton, who told me and Donley. We still sat enthralled weekday afternoons after school, watching the radio as we listened to another chapter of Terry and the Pirates, but at the commercial breaks, one of us would ask Luke, "How much more?" because the clinking of his counted coins was a constant counterpoint to the radio drama.

And finally one day he flashed his big-toothed grin and answered, "No more. I have all I need. I'm going to get that gun tomorrow after school."

We restrained our cheering in the interest of keeping the secret from the element of the family who would without doubt disapprove of the venture.

The four of us discussed tactics on the way to school the next morning. Carrington had gone on to high school and Martin and Vala were just barely too young to accompany us to St. A's. We would have liked to go in a body to Weil's Sporting Goods and witness the purchase. But for all four of us to arrive late at home would attract unwanted notice, and Mother, if she got worried, was not above calling the nuns to inquire as to our whereabouts.

So we three agreed we would cover for Luke by inventing an excuse—and here it was established that one excuse would be universally used, not like on earlier occasions when three different conspirators came up with three different excuses, again causing the spotlight of parental disapproval to settle on our guilty selves.

Then, when Luke got home, he would slink up through the apple trees and cache the gun in the hayloft, a place reasonably safe from search and seizure, and it would not be until tomorrow that we would all take our eyesight, if not our very lives, into our hands to try out the new toy.

So it was done. With a display of histrionic talent, Trent tossed his books on the table, hotly exclaiming to our mother that the unfair nuns, hiding their hypocrisy behind their veils, had unfairly accused Luke of some act for which he was patently innocent and had kept him after school. And he had especially wanted to know what happened to Sky King today.

The following day was very long. The hour hand on the clock moved with heretofore-unknown sluggishness, but even geography and history must come to an end, and so they did that day. Once we made an appearance at home and spoke to Mother to let her know we were home from school, we made our separate ways to the grove of apple trees where Luke magnanimously allowed us to take turns firing his BB gun.

And after all, it was not really so much fun. You aimed the gun, sighting along the barrel by squinting one eye and having discovered the object for which you decided to aim, pulled the trigger, invariably missing the target by such a margin as to be immeasurable. Gamely, I took my turns, noticing that none of the other three seemed disappointed. And after my fifth turn I realized why. Luke, having missed everything in the world the first few times, then hit a tree, then a particular branch, and toward the end of the session, good size rocks on the ground. Trent did only a little worse and Donley about the same as Trent. While I, again and again, merely made ripples in the air by BBs falling harmlessly to the ground, lost among the high grasses.

It was the same old story of the baseball games in which I never scored the winning run. It was the games of Red Rover all over again when I was always the first one to be called right over, only to be added willy-nilly to the line of the opposing team so frequently in the course of a game that my loyalties were hopelessly confused. It was just like the games of Kick the Can when I hid behind the line of Aunt Petty's yellow rose bushes because they smelled so good and was the first one found. Then I was forced to be "It" for the rest of the evening because every time I caught somebody, somebody else kicked the damned can.

"Dammit," I said, but too low for anyone else to hear. That felt pretty good, so I walked a little further from the rest of them and said it again.

I had never cussed outside in the open before, only in the chicken house where the noise made it less than satisfying. I gave a good kick at an apple tree and said it once more. Damn it to hell anyway. In this enormous family, I alone after eleven years of life had not achieved outstanding status at anything. Perhaps I could excel at cussing.

"Time to go, Digger," they called to me and I could see they were right, so I abandoned my cussing practice and we all walked back along the path together until Luke branched off to the barn to put the gun back in its hiding place.

We must have practiced four nights a week all through the rest of the early spring. Luke seemed to have a real talent for shooting, but even Trent and Donley began to show signs of proficiency. I only went along down to the apple trees because I was so much in the habit of seeking their company that to be listening to the serials on the radio would have been infinitely worse than dragging along.

"I guess I'll just skip my turns tonight," I offered, and the other three generously accepted my sacrifice. Even cussing was beginning to lose its charm as I became full time thrower-upper of tin cans and clumps of clayey soil for the others to shoot at, cringing back immediately when the object left my hand lest their aim be as poor as my own. I kept in mind the havoc a BB gun was reputed to wreak. And then all of a sudden, it quit being fun for all of us. Not only was I bored with the game, but also the other three. You can only climb so many mountains, swim so many oceans, fire so many BBs before the excitement begins to pall, and thus it was with us. Other pursuits claimed our attention. The BB gun lay in isolation for days at a time in the hayloft.

Occasionally, the boys would go out together and take potshots at whatever drew their eyes, and on one such occasion, Luke, just seeing if he could, aimed at and brought down one of the wild canaries that inhabited the grove of apple trees. He was horrified at what he had done, but even worse, there was a witness to the atrocity.

"What do you think you're doing?" The voice from behind him nearly turned Luke's golden hair silver. Conner reached over his younger brother's shoulder and tore the

BB gun from his loose grasp. "Don't you know that's a songbird?" Conner reached down and picked up the body of evidence. "You're going to march right back to the house and tell Mom what you've done."

All my life, and this was no exception, I wondered why God had seen fit to have us middle Mosses live out our childhood surrounded on every side by tattletales.

There was simply no sense arguing. Conner was much heavier, much taller, and much broader than Luke. Luke suffered himself to be dragged houseward. Donley and I were down at the barn when the three-man procession passed and fell in behind to see what was happening. Reaching the kitchen, where Mother was busy kneading bread dough, Conner tossed the dead bird down on the table and delivered the culprit over for speedy retribution.

Chickens were routinely beheaded before our very eyes all the time, and we had never reacted with any degree of horror to the sight. The dead bird, though a good deal more picturesque than the chickens, still aroused no great passion of wrath in me as it apparently did for Conner, but simply a sadness for beauty inadvertently lost. I thought Conner was being his usual officious self.

Mother stood by, prepared to intervene as soon as she knew what was going on, but reluctant to wash her hands of the dough before she had finished kneading it. Conner pulled Luke around to face him and accused him.

"Don't you know that's a songbird you killed?"

Of course Luke knew. For one thing, Conner had just told him it was. Besides, it was a reflex action, one which Luke regretted the minute it was too late for regret. Had

Conner been less authoritative, Luke might have wept for the destruction of the small bird, colored so much like himself. But he couldn't say so, not now.

"I wouldn't be surprised but that's against the law, what you did." Conner was going on.

"Well, why don't you just call the police and have me arrested?" Luke sneered.

"Arrested! I guess not, but for two cents, I'd knock your block off!"

Luke compressed his lips over the retort that hung there and shoved one hand into his trouser pocket and withdrawing it, flung two copper coins on the floor.

"Okay, blowhard, there's two cents."

Conner's swing was as reflexive as Luke's action earlier had been. Just as Mother stepped forward to intervene, Conner brought his fist back and unleashed a mighty swing at his younger brother. All his life we referred to Luke as Lucas Joseph Duck, and at that moment, he gave us reason to remember the old nickname. He ducked low to avoid the blow that Conner had telegraphed so clearly and Conner missed him completely.

Mother's reflexes were not quick enough, not as quick as Luke's. When she stepped forward, she had stepped right into the path of the blow, and Conner connected mightily. Her glasses broke and fell to the floor, and she covered her face with both of her hands.

"Son of a damned-to-hell bitch," I said, my cussing practice standing me in good stead at a time when strong language seemed called for. No one even noticed.

The kitchen was full of people by now, the entire family attracted by Conner's shouting. We were horrified to see blood trickling through Mother's fingers. We stood paralyzed by our horror until Ragan stepped forward to draw Mother's hands away from her face and disclose, just below the left eye, a small triangular cut from which bright red blood gushed as if a vein had been cut.

Trent sensibly moved the bread dough from harm's way, and Donley stooped to recover Mother's shattered glasses. Conner and Luke stared at each other, trying to assess the degree of blame the other should bear.

It took long minutes to be sure that besides her broken glasses, Mother's sight was not adversely affected and the cut looked infinitely worse than it was. Even as our relieved chatter burst into the silence, it became apparent that Mother would have the black eye to end all black eyes.

"Don't talk to me about what's against the law and what's not," Luke snarled at Conner. "You hit your own mother."

Poor Conner. He blustered and muttered that it had not been his fault, but his air of officiousness melted away, leaving him shriveled before our very eyes. Hi didn't even have the relief of saying how sorry he was because to apologize meant accepting the blame.

Mother bore her "shiner" with good humor. I heard her tell an acquaintance, lightheartedly, that it was the result of a marital dispute. "You should see the other guy," she would say.

But when Pop heard her repeat the remark, having gotten a laugh the first time, he didn't see the humor at all. He found excuses for her to stay indoors, even going so far as to grocery shop himself until the bruising faded. Sunday mass was the sole exception, and she wore a heavy veil and a lot of powder for that.

But I guess all they say about BB guns is true. They do cause eye damage.

Chapter Thirteen

Mr. Elston came over to say that he had put the acreage adjoining our own on the market. Banished from the kitchen, as we always were when adults dropped by for a cup of coffee and some grownup talk, we listened below the kitchen window to see if Mr. Elston was blaming us for the sale. Had he found out that it was we who had dammed the stream with stones and logs and a mortar of clayey soil to create a swimming pool, succeeding beyond our own ambitions and in the process wiping out two partial rows of his soy beans? Had somebody told him that we played hide and seek in his asparagus fronds after the cutting season was over and hadn't done the asparagus any good? Or perhaps it had come to his notice that Luke's friend visited on his motorcycle, and when Mother said explicitly that under no circumstances was Luke to try to ride it, we had taken it into the rows of tall corn to escape detection? The corn had not benefited noticeably any more than the asparagus, but we had all gone out later and propped up any stalks we found leaning over, bringing excess clods of dirt to shore them up at the foundation line.

But no, Mr. Elston had come with no enmity at all. He simply had gotten too old, he told Mom and Pop, to keep on with the backbreaking labor inherent in market gardening. We agreed with his choice of adjectives.

"It's different for you, Moss. You have all these youngsters who take an interest."

Interest, indeed! Without the persuasion of my parents' forceful personalities, you couldn't have caught me within ten feet of a tomato plant or a hoe. Mr. and Mrs. Elston were considering retirement in Florida, where their only son had gone to live years ago. They sure would miss the Mosses, he said, and I appreciated him saying it, particularly because he didn't add that you also miss a rock when you take it out of your shoe.

A realtor's sign went up, the Elstons left, and I grew accustomed to seeing the ground given over to nothing more worthwhile than ragweed and cottonweed, with the occasional sunflower thrusting cheerfully up past the flourishing weeds to beam full-faced at the world.

Until one day there was activity: a tractor, barely bigger than the one Pop owned but equipped with a frontal attached device that took gulps out of the dirt, was chewing a hole in the ground, less than a city block from our own driveway. We all made our way through the weeds to watch. Day after fall day, the hole in the ground became a basement, and on top of it, a structure became recognizable as a house. A house means people, and we watched and waited once more to try to catch sight of whoever it might be. After the workmen left each day, we moved in to walk off the rooms of the house (only four of them) and came to a conclusion about their size: small. All this ground and such a little house. We sure felt sorry for anybody who had to live here and hoe all the surrounding acres. It was obvious there wouldn't be enough of them to divide the work up.

And finally one day, taking the long way home from school to bring us unobtrusively past the house, Donley and I saw the lady. She looked very young, dressed in slacks (our mother never dressed in slacks) with her hair draped attractively over her forehead and curling behind her ears (our mother never had her hair done). Her eyes were made larger by the expert application of eye shadow and mascara, and her lips bloomed under a light layer of pale red lipstick (our mother never wore makeup.) We decided she couldn't possibly be the mother.

Wrong again. She called to us to come talk to her, and we cheerfully and instantly obliged. We told her our names and ages, pointed out the house we lived in, and reeled off the ages of our brothers and sisters. She was probably enthralled.

"I have a boy about your age."

We weren't sure if she meant my age or Donley's, but perhaps she meant both. After all, Donley and I weren't all that far removed from each other in years.

I tried to hide my disappointment about the number and sex of her child. I had been hoping that there would be friends for all of us.

"His name is Walter," she invited us with her smile to consider that name. "His father was named Walter is why."

We were all the way home before it occurred to us that she had spoken of Walter's father, Walter, in the past tense, which probably meant that he wasn't around, maybe even dead. We felt sorry, and therefore ready to like the younger Walter before we even met him. That happened the next day.

Right after school, Donley and I put on our roller skates and just happened to choose to skate on the tarred road that led past the new house. After we had skated back and forth a few times, maybe a hundred, lo and behold! A car pulled up into the space that would become front yard and decanted a boy smaller than Donley and only a little taller than I. I was sure glad to see him, because it meant I could take off my roller skates and rest my poor legs. Sturdy as they were, my legs were never as strong as my curiosity, and all that roller-skating was wearing me out.

"Aren't those neat skates?' Walter said politely as he saw me take them off. "They scoot back and forth so they would fit you no matter how much your feet grow. I only have shoe skates."

In exchange for the information we had given his mother the day before, Walter told us that his father was indeed departed from this life, having been a soldier who died in the line of duty, that he went to a public school—Graham—but expected to transfer next September to somewhere closer, perhaps St. A's. Maybe he could go to school with us. Also we found out that he was two months younger that I, but because his birthday fell so late in the year, he had been kept back at home for a year and was thus a year behind me in school. He was studying very hard with the hope that he would be allowed to skip sixth grade. Furthermore, his mother, though widowed, did not work and did not intend to garden this land because Walter's grandparents thought it was more important that she stay home with Walter because he had been sick when he was a baby and even last year had spent some time in the hospital, though he was okay now.

Nothing Walter told us, though, impressed me as much as the shoe skates. I had wanted shoe skates all my life; I was born hoping for them. I was absolutely certain that given shiny, white high-topped shoe skates that supported my ankles, I would not only be a truly great skater, but a skater to rival Sonja Henie, who was the model for paper dolls and did other swell, remunerative-type things. I was also certain that I would keep them clean at all times, far cleaner than I ever managed to keep my unfortunately smudged and scraped saddle shoes. Shoe skates, in a sentence, would firm up both my ability and my character. And here was Walter who actually possessed such skates—though his were probably brown or black—admiring the ingenuity of my adjustable framework-type of skates. Walter was indubitably one of nature's noblemen.

Walter also had a bike, shiny new, which he compared to my brothers to the disadvantage of his own.

"Gee, I'll bet without fenders and a chain guard, that bike's really light. I'll bet you can really go fast on that bike."

Walter's was the first bike I had ever seen actually in the possession of a person, as opposed to a hardware store, that was still painted its original color and had fenders as well. Although he went to public school, he walked with us for the first six blocks before branching off. We studied his school books, which were in mint condition, having both covers and all pages intact just as they had come from the printers, with only his name neatly penciled on the first page. I did not own a schoolbook except those, which, like my clothes, were handed down. Many of them had the name of every one of my older brothers and sisters written on the flyleaf, if indeed the flyleaf was intact, only to be crossed out a year later and the new owner's name inscribed—on and on, ad infinitum.

"Boy, that's sure neat," Walter said of my books. "I'll bet you can get all kinds of help with your homework if all those guys used this same book."

My brothers at first treated Walter like a cross between the plague and cousin Anne Louise. Anne Louise was also an only child of two working parents and also had all kinds of things we wished we had. The difference, I kept pointing out to Trent and Luke, was that Anne Louise gloated over us. At a time in our lives when Donley would have cheerfully sold off her hope of heaven for gymnastic lessons, Anne Louise complained that her mother forced her to join the class. On a Saturday afternoon, she demonstrated what she had learned in gymnastics class by hanging by her fingers from the high railing of the back porch. Trent grabbed up a hammer and tapped her smartly across the fingers of the right hand. Anne Louise deserved that. When Trent said, "Sorry, I must have hit the wrong nail," we all laughed in spite of Anne Louise's tears of pain and rage. When she had gone to tell on us, Luke spotted the shiny new, white purse she brought with her: a purse empty except for those accoutrements it had come with—mirror and coin purse—and slung it in the stream where the water was deepest and denied ever having seen it. Anne Louise deserved that, too.

But Walter was different.

"Digger's got a boyfriend," said Trent and Luke, and they tittered and giggled all the rest of the way to the movies, so I gave up trying to make them see that Walter was a really nice person and deserved better than that at their hands.

On weekends, Walter came over to play and brought the shoe skates. He thought maybe there would be somewhere we could skate at our house. His mom had a headache, or we could skate in their cellar that had a concrete floor. Our own had a brick floor, and Sonja herself would have been hard put to remain upright down there. With the road covered with ice and dirtied snow, the only place I could think of was the hayloft, so Donley and I found our lesser breed of roller skates, and we all went down to the barn. The hayloft extended over half of the barn and was reached by climbing a short ladder mounted against the wall. I had no head for heights and clung for dear life to the rungs as I climbed. When I thrust my head and body through the hole in the hayloft floor and scrambled up, I never looked down, although it was only about eight feet to the barn floor.

Donley and I made a barricade of hay bales across the open end of the loft so we could skate the length of it and turn without putting ourselves in danger of going over the unrailed edge. We explained all this to Walter, who put on the shoe skates and doggedly tried our method. I must have been wrong about the magical properties of shoe skates, because Walter was worse than I was. In fact, Walter had never skated before and skated as if that were the case.

"Well, I was sick last year, and before that I guess I was too young."

Maybe it was only white skates that made the wearer so expert. Poor Walter never learned all day to stop short of the hay bales, but time after time, plowed right into the barrier before he could stop himself. But he said he had a good time and when Donley said, "Digger, we better go in for lunch," Walter said he sure wished he had a nickname. He thought Digger was a really great name, a fun type thing to be called.

That same week when Donley and I, with several other girlfriends, were enroute from school, our path joined the homeward way of a group of kids from Graham School that included Walter. He immediately deserted that group to join us. From the group of Grahamites, somebody called out that Walter was walking with the "Mossy Tombstone Kids," for the name had caught on and we would be destined to hear it all our school days. Walter erupted out of our group and shot across to punch the offender. We were nearly as surprised as the boy, who had to pick himself off the ground, the nickname having lost any sting by becoming so familiar.

Understandably, the punchee was offended enough to come off the ground swinging at Walter, an action serving to incite all his companions into wanting nothing so much as to take a swing themselves. It was not in our natures to remain uninvolved, so we joined in the fray—St. A's was far from being a finishing school—and gave as good or maybe a lot better than we got. We saved Walter from a massacre at the hands of his schoolmates. And when our friends said slyly that Donley and I had acquired a champion, I didn't mind nearly as much as I minded my brothers' teasing.

Early in December, Mrs. Rector stopped by to ask if several of us would consent to help her and Walter decorate the house for Christmas. She was hesitant to come in the house, not wanting to impose, but once coaxed in for a cup of coffee and a taste of Mom's fruitcake, she talked with such eagerness as to betray her longing for conversation.

Her parents, we learned, had gone south to live, and indeed it was on a visit to them that she had met the Elstons and learned about the property for sale. The doctor wasn't sure, but she was, that Walter needed only fresh air, unpolluted and in quantity, to restore him to health.

"Just look at Odell, how healthy and robust she is."

I wasn't sure I was being complimented. Furthermore, she felt that her opinion was being confirmed.

We were invited to look how Walter's skin glowed, and he had gained seven pounds. A discomfited Walter allowed his skin to be inspected for glowiness and his frame to be assessed for the distribution of the extra pounds.

But there now, she was talking too much about herself and her own ideas. She would love to hear whatever Mrs. Moss could tell her about the city's schools, shops, whatever. Since Christmas was not far off, Mrs. Rector—call me Alice—would be making any number of excursions to town and if there was anything she could bring Mrs. Moss or perhaps if Mrs. Moss needed a lift into town. Mother thanked her politely and said she'd see, which meant no. Mother saw Mrs. Rector off with a generous helping of fruitcake for her supper and said Walter was welcome over any time.

The Rectors' Christmas tree was a revelation to me. It looked like an illustration from a Currier and Ives card. Of course, we were used to Christmas trees. We never failed to have one, but Pop put off the actual moment of buying one until the last Saturday before Christmas Eve, which could be the twenty-third some years, and he had a very low limit on the sum that went toward its purchase. Consequently, our trees tended to be spindly. Last year, Pop had picked out the tree all by himself, and while it was plenty slim enough to fit comfortably into a corner without disruption of the everyday arrangement of furniture, it was much too tall for our ten-foot ceiling. He lopped off the top three feet of the tree in order for it to stand up in the room. Donley and I took the top three feet to our own room, where we stuck it in a fruit jar filled with wet sand and decorated it with half a dozen discarded ornaments and a few strands of pilfered tinsel. There was little to choose between the family tree and our own.

Chapter Thirteen

The Rectors' tree had come from a local florist and had been carried into the house and set into a stand before we arrived. It had been lightly coated with artificial snow and the florist had even strung lights cunningly so that blue, green, and red lights winked on the whiteness of the treated branches without a wire to be seen. Heck! Sometimes we had to hang ornaments on those wires and tinsel them in order to make our tree look festive, short of branches as it sometimes was. It dawned on me that Mrs. Rector asked for us less for her need of help than as an excuse for a small party to brighten the rather lonely holiday for Walter. Hot chocolate, topped with rich blobs of whipped cream, accompanied bakery cookies.

Clever Alice Rector realized that home-baked goodies held no excitement for us. Perhaps the star shapes, the Santa Claus faces, and the reindeer lacked the rich taste of our mother's, but the icing so painstakingly used to create the cookies enchanted us. Good thing Pop wasn't there to ponder on the ill effects of food coloring. He regarded bakery cookies with the same misgiving he held toward carnival grounds hot dogs.

I assumed it was the Rectors' first tree because there were brand new boxes of tinsel to put on it, and that too was something I wasn't used to. Our own mother saved the tinsel from year to year. It isn't all that difficult to smooth out used tinsel and decorate a tree with it, but it's a mean job to pick it off the spindly, dry branches of a used-up Christmas tree and store it.

Mrs. Rector had small gifts for us too: coloring books for Vala, a rubber ball for Martin, handkerchiefs for me, toilet water for Donley. We were awed by such generosity. I didn't see how anybody could make toilet water.

Just three days later, when Christmas excitement was at a peak, Walter again came over to skate in our hayloft. His mother felt fine today, but he thought it was more fun at our house. Back to the hayloft we climbed. Someone had used up the bales of hay we used as a barrier, so we skated the other direction. The floor was laid in planks of wood that after many years tended to cup slightly in the center, making the floor look a little like a child's illustration of a wavy ocean. We opted to skate with the grain of the wood. Donley and I offered to shove a few more bales of hay in front of the spot where the floor ended and space began, but Walter said no, he'd mastered his skates by now. And indeed the first two swoops across the wooden floor, with the noise echoing around the half empty barn adding to our own enthusiastic vocal efforts, Walter managed to turn gracefully and stop before he reached the edge. I don't know what happened the third time. He simply did not stop, but went sailing past the edge of the floor, and when Donley and I looked over the edge, he lay on the barn floor trying valiantly to smile, but his face was shockingly pale.

I thought that Mrs. Rector would demand back her Christmas presents when she came to take Walter for x-rays, for she was very nearly distraught, but she did not. In fact, she made it a point to stop by on her way home, Walter left in the car, displaying a snow white sling with an air of pride, to assure us that accidents happen (we knew that) and no blame was attached to anyone. She hinted that we might do our skating the rest of the winter on the stream, because Walter was hoping for ice skates. I didn't think much of the idea because I had hoped for ice skates for years myself and never got any. While Walter might have more success with his Christmas hoping, still he had his arm in that sling.

All through the winter and the spring, Walter joined us in our games, replacing Luke, who, now that he was in high school, refused to join in the foolishness perpetrated by the grade school crowd. One day in March, Walter told us that when September rolled around, he would be attending St. Albert's as a seventh grader. Walter's knowledge of geography and math was prodigious, and his history sufficient to allow him, as he had hoped, to skip sixth grade.

"Digger and I will be in the same class."

But I knew we never would. I never managed to get out of the "average" class in my grade, and I knew Walter would be a star.

The boiler at school broke on a bitterly cold day the last day of March and resulted in an unofficial day off school for us, so we were home when Mrs. Rector came to call on Mother. It was apparent that she was disturbed about something. As always, Mother shooed us away, and Donley and I went upstairs to listen at the grille in the floor of our room, which allowed heat from the kitchen, not to mention news of the day's events, to flow upward to our room.

Mrs. Rector's voice was so soft that Donley and I could hardly hear, so we delicately, carefully lifted out the top half of the grille in order to be able to take turns lowering our listening ears below the surface of the floor to hear better. By the time we tuned in, it was obvious that Mrs. Rector was well launched on her subject, and from the ease with which Mother's answers came, it was equally obvious that the subject was one they had discussed before: Walter's health or lack of the same. Mother was reassuring Mrs. Rector that Walter looked fine to her, and if the doctor thought he was improved, then you could count on it, the boy was fine. Mother's words acted on Mrs. Rector as the sun affects the morning glory, and before Mother poured a second cup of coffee, Walter's mother was soothed.

"You know, Alice," Mother said, passing the cream and sugar, "your worrying and fussing are probably the worst things Walter has to contend with."

That line also bore the sound of familiarity, and when Mrs. Rector answered, "Yes, I know, but Walter's all I have," we thought she had probably said that before.

We abandoned our listening post in disgust. It was impossible to return the top half of the grille to position without being heard below, so we shoved that part beneath the bed and covered the resultant hole with a throw rug.

Two days later, poor Carrington, coming into our room to look for a safety pin, stepped unaware on the throw rug, which naturally gave under her and plunged her—or at least her whole right leg—through the bottom half of the grille and through the kitchen ceiling. Our brothers made much of Carrie's showing off her legs, but I like to think that if she had been hurt, they might not have. Or again, they might. My pop often said that if you want to make the Irish laugh, fall off your chair, which led to my mother passing remarks about the English.

Pop plastered over the hole, and we never heard another thing that took place in the kitchen nor did the smell of bacon ever again waft up to us, waking us pleasurably. Life is full of sorrowful happenings.

It took a long time for the school year to wind down and release us to summer pleasures. For the last month we seemed to spend our arithmetic abilities counting days, minutes, and seconds. We made plans to dam up the stream again, since soy beans no longer grew in the path of danger. We talked about building a tree house to replace the one that was falling apart in the big mulberry tree. Walter asked if he could come over and help with the canning. It sounded like fun to him: Walter found fun where the rest of us saw drudgery.

But when the canning season was upon us, not only was Walter not allowed to help, our cousins could not come over either. I realized that Walter had been right, and I wrong. Canning season was fun when the work was shared. With only ourselves, it was hard work, and without Aunt Petty, Mother was irritable. The summer I had looked forward to with so much enthusiasm was utterly ruined because of the Health Department.

Polio was a word I hadn't even heard before that summer. And when I first heard it, I thought of a game played on horseback, but polio was no game. When reported cases reached epidemic proportions, I learned a second word: quarantine.

The health authorities decided that people between infancy and middle teens were most vulnerable and asked all parents to keep at home those children who fell within that age bracket. The local swimming pool was closed, and we never got a chance to open the one we planned at the bottom of the hill.

The only bright spot as far as we were concerned was that Mother decreed that staying at home meant just that, and our trips to Sunday Mass were curtailed. For six weeks, we heard neither sermon nor choir. It was absolutely splendid. In order to keep holy the Sabbath, Mother further decreed that we should all join in the saying of the rosary. We would wait until she and Pop had left for church and then launched on the fastest rosary ever recorded by man. Probably it was not recorded in eternity. After all, we were young and God was infinitely merciful.

And our sufferings were as nothing compared to Walter's. For the first time, when looking across the fields to spot Walter riding his fancy bike around the house on the walks and up and down the graveled drive, I realized how lonely an only child can be. At least once a day, we called him on the telephone, but Walter, left to his own devices, was dull and had nothing to say. He didn't want to listen either, because our activities, limited though they were, made him a little envious.

Carter showed us how two tin cans joined by wire could make an instrument of communication of sorts, and he strung such a device between our two houses. For a couple of days, Walter was an enthusiastic user of this primitive telephone, but after that, he found it no better than the Bell system. If you have nothing to say, you have nothing to say, regardless of the sophistication of your equipment.

Chapter Thirteen

Poor Walter. At first, his absence was keenly felt, but in the nature of things, the gap was slowly but inevitably closed as we turned to each other for company even more than we had been used to. For another week, Donley and I wrote notes and had the mailman deliver them as he passed Walter's box, but Walter had to use a stamp to carry his return notes and soon gave up replying. And when our notes were not reciprocated, we quit writing them. Our sole means of reaching out toward Walter was a wave as we spotted him across the fields.

Meantime, the news from in town became worse. A clerk from the bank fell sick on a Tuesday and died on Saturday. One of the Clarke children died suddenly before her parents realized that she was even ill. The older of the Morley twins was stricken and lay for a week in an iron lung before he too died. And two girls from school lost partial use of a leg or an arm with a "light" case of the illness.

One Friday, Walter rang through on the tin can telephone by the simple expedient of banging a hammer against a sturdy piece of metal. He was happier than we had heard him all summer. His mother had heard that the epidemic was under control and had promised him an outing. They were going out to dinner and a movie that very night. Our sympathy for Walter evaporated. We had never been taken out to dinner in our lives, and we asked dozens of questions about the choice of restaurant and menu. When we saw the car pass our house, we waved exuberantly and pulled what we thought were funny faces to show Walter that we were envious. We comforted ourselves that if the quarantine was indeed lifted, Walter would soon be back to play.

On Saturday, Walter called on the telephone. An unaccustomed night out had worn him out, he joked. Since he hadn't left the house for so long, he wasn't used to being out in such a heady atmosphere for so long, but he'd had a good time and he told us all about the meal and the plot of the movie. The phone conversation took almost forty minutes.

On Sunday, Donley and I called Walter, but his mother said he was sleeping, and we failed to hear the worry in her voice. On Sunday night, we were awakened by the sound of a siren and came downstairs, half dressed, to peer out into the night. The Rectors' house was the only one we could see, and our eyes were drawn to it by the sight of a red light, turning and turning, flashing toward us and away again. The siren was muted, as if it were an animal that, having sighted its quarry, need no longer speed in full cry. We didn't need Mrs. Rector's phone call the following morning to tell us that Walter was in the hospital.

We all prayed, not the hurried prayers with words tumbling over each other that our weekly rosaries had been, but fervent prayers spoken low, to reach heaven all the faster.

Walter died on Thursday.

The hospital called us at the request of Walter's grandparents, who had hurried up from Florida but who were themselves unable to relay the news. We pleaded to be allowed to attend the funeral, but Mother was adamant. We saw Mrs. Rector come home from it, driven by her father, all three of them—Mrs. Rector, her mother, and her father—sitting upright in the seat, looking straight ahead. Such a small funeral it must have been. We stood on the porch as the car passed, hoping Mrs. Rector could read the grief in our faces and be comforted by it, but she never once turned to look in our direction.

Mother wept hardest of all and my pop, for the first time put his arms around her in public—at least as public as our kitchen was. Mother wept mostly for Mrs. Rector, because she was as sure as only a good woman can be of Walter's eternal well being. And she wept for herself too, torn between her need to go to comfort a bereaved parent and her fear of contaminating her own children.

The quarantine was lifted the following week, but somehow there wasn't any place I wanted to go anymore.

We never saw Mrs. Rector again. The day of the funeral, she packed her things and went back to Florida with her parents. The weeds grew higher than ever on the empty acreage, nature striving to reclaim for its own what Mrs. Rector had tried to tame. It stayed empty until two years later, when a moving van could be seen at the house and even from the distance of our bedroom windows, the moving figures had a vague familiarity. That afternoon, Mr. Elston appeared in our kitchen to say that retirement and a sunny climate were not enough to make a life. He had bought back his fields from Mrs. Rector and would try his hand at market gardening again. With the house right on the property, he thought that he and Mrs. Elston between them could handle things. We were glad to have them back in the neighborhood.

Another year passed before Mrs. Elston told us that she had heard from Mrs. Rector's mother. Mrs. Rector had married and a new baby was expected. I was torn by the news. I wanted Mrs. Rector to be happy, but I didn't like the idea that she would be somebody else's mother—somebody beside Walter. And then it occurred to me that Walter would have been pleased, so I was too. I hope the new baby was half as nice as Walter.

Chapter Fourteen

Our old house, I had been told, had been built by a one-armed man. On lazy summer afternoons, I lay along the fat branch of a mulberry tree and tried to visualize him, poor man, driving a nail. Later I found out that what they meant was that the house had been commissioned to be built by a gentleman who had lost an arm. Some knowledge is unnecessary and even harmful.

Up to the time I heard the explanation, I knew why our house had certain eccentricities—it all came back to the difficulties a one-armed man encountered in a world of two-armed people. The heat, for instance. The house was heated by a huge monster of a furnace that burned coal. A great deal of coal, Pop always said. No heat ran to the bedroom that my parents occupied off the kitchen—the theory being, I suppose, that the kitchen heat would leak through and warm it adequately. After all, how much heat do you need when you are sleeping beneath three rag-pieced quilts? The kitchen itself had little excess heat in spite of the heating stove that was supposed to provide auxiliary heat during the bitter winter months, possibly because seven doors and two windows allowed the cold air to come in. There was one door each to the basement, dining room, living room, pantry, the aforementioned bedroom, the side porch-turned-music room, and the back yard. So four of the seven doors opened into spaces colder than the kitchen itself.

Every morning in winter, we would come shivering from our own unheated bedrooms, take our plates of scrambled eggs (good mornings) or bowls of oatmeal (bad mornings) and find a place to warm ourselves around the heating stove. It was a big enough stove, as stoves go, but still didn't have enough circumference to allow each of us a place. We made toast by applying slices of bread to the back of the stove. Yes, of course we had a toaster, but only used it in the summer. It only made two slices at a time, and besides, electricity costs money, we were given to understand. The entire back of the stove was lettered with the brand name of the stove (Oxtrong), its place of origin, and other pertinent information. Mother disapproved of cold, boxed cereals for breakfast. She believed that when they shot them out of a gun, they left all the nutrients in the air, so even though we never entertained ourselves at breakfast by reading the cereal box, we could read our toast.

"Patent pending…Oxtrong Stoves…Since 1879…," said our toast in browned letters. It was better to read it before you buttered and jellied it.

Looking back from the vantage point of years gone by, I wonder that all that humanity did not warm the kitchen, but it most emphatically did not. From mid-October until mid-April, Mother wore one or another of a selection of moth-eaten, disreputable old sweaters she kept on hooks behind the pantry door. Anyone surveying the garments hung on those hooks would have reached the reasonable assumption that we were either eagerly awaiting the arrival of the rag buyer or just entertained a very persuasive rag seller. I still couldn't say where all the outerwear had its origin. God knows we recycled our clothing, but that was ridiculous. Mother only removed her day's choice of sweater when she heard company coming. I wonder how many times she was embarrassed to be caught dressed like the scullery maid on those times when company arrived silently.

One April morning, we were dismantling the stove and listening to the radio. This was so much handier than today's television since your eyes were not necessarily involved and you were free to turn up the volume and go about your business. The radio discussion was about the use of color to make a room appear larger, warmer, or lighter. We already knew how to make it look smaller. Those old walls must have had fifty coats of paint, and if you figure the thickness of one coat...but never mind. Turquoise and aquamarine make a room seem cooler, a very cool voice was informing us and being agreed with by a heavy, masculine voice. And weren't browns and yellows warm colors? The subject was batted back and forth for several minutes before Mother pointed out that perhaps the blue paint of the kitchen added something to the chill factor. A sunbeam danced off the blue and made me think of ice caught in the glare of winter sunshine. I thought Mother was probably right.

Again from the vantage point of greater knowledge, I suspect what the kitchen needed was weather-stripping and storm doors, but those things cost cash, something we were chronically short of.

The conversation must have planted a seed in Carrington's mind, and it took about two weeks to germinate. We were discussing a suitable gift for Mother's Day, and for suitable, read inexpensive. Last Mother's Day we had filled an old sauerkraut crock with dirt and planted it with broken plants we had bought cheap from the friendly florist. It had been a great hit: the flowers under Mother's loving care soon overcame their early handicap and the crock was the envy of Aunt Petty for the entire summer. But of course, it was difficult to see how, having achieved such a hit last year, we were to follow that particular act.

"I know what we can do." Carrington spoke softly, but received instant attention. If she knew something we could "do" as opposed to "buy" for a gift, we were ready to give her a hearing. "We can paint the kitchen."

Paint the kitchen? I wished we hadn't invited Carrington to express herself on the matter of a gift. If we all went in together, Carrington pointed out, we could afford to buy at least two gallons of paint. There were brushes in the cellar from earlier painting jobs, and we could do the work on the Saturday before Mother's Day when Mother and Pop would be going to visit our Moss grandparents.

"I have a gift for Mother's Day. I bought it myself." Ragan said, disassociating herself from the project before it became reality. Pressed, she refused to say the nature of her choice for a gift, and I suspected that Ragan simply didn't want to get involved with the work of painting the kitchen. I can't say I was looking forward to it.

"How are you going to get two gallons of paint home? Carry it on your bike?" Ragan was skeptical, as well as critical. "And what color are you going to get? You can't know what color Mother would like the kitchen painted."

But Carrington did know. Mother wanted the warmest color possible; we had all heard her say it herself.

"I'll leave you to the planning since I won't be a party to this." Ragan got up from the stair on which she had been sitting and stalked off.

I wasn't sorry to see her go. I was of the firm opinion that Ragan had been spoiled back in those dimly distant days when the family had numbered so many fewer children than today, and she had been the only daughter.

She was undeniably a pet. There can be more pets than one in the family and at present, ours numbered two: Ragan and Vala. I liked my mother and all that, but it was increasingly difficult for me to understand why, given a kid like me, as nice a kid as ever avoided the cracks in the pavement in order to preserve a mother's health, she continued to favor the likes of Vala and Ragan. But there is simply no accounting for tastes.

We worked out the plan among the five of us. Neither Carter nor Conner were home and both Vala and Martin were too little to help with the work, so we did not take them into our confidence.

We knew all about painting, of course. I think that as we left the crib, our fairy godmothers in the dark of a black night came all unaware and substituted a paint brush in the hand that had been used to a rattle, and we had been helping with beautification projects ever since.

I can still remember the spring when Mother decided that beneath the paint on the rail and balusters of the stairway lay golden oak which stripped and polished would look much lovelier than the white enamel that graced them at that time. She bought one very small can of paint stripper and a truckload of sandpaper and set us to work removing generations of paint. She pointed out what a fine and rare opportunity it would provide for us to see the different tastes evidenced by each succeeding strata of color and set us to work. She herself dabbed on just a soupcon of paint remover and we, by dint of elbow grease and determination, removed forty hundred layers of paint. They were all white. That was another project Ragan managed to avoid.

When the balustrades and rail were laid bare, it became apparent that the golden oak had been just myth and white pine was the actual material that had formed them. Regretfully, Mother bought a couple of quarts of white enamel, and we painted the splotchy, irregular wood so that it looked nearly as good as it had before we started.

And we painted the bedrooms a lot. There were five of them, four opening off an upstairs landing just big enough to stand on and decide which direction you wanted to go. The room I shared with Donley and Vala had sloping walls following the line of the roof so that the outside walls only rose about four feet vertically and then began to slope sharply upwards. If you were over three and a half feet tall, you were only really comfortable in the very center of the room. Donley and I had to paint that room the week after Christmas because some well-intentioned person had gifted Vala with a large box of crayons and no coloring book and the child had needed somewhere to try out the various colors. It is very difficult to paint over wax crayon markings.

The room now looked a little strange to the unfamiliar eye. We had chosen a mint green, and Mom had calculated to a nicety the amount of paint it would take and bought that much. Unfortunately, her measurements always tended to be skimpy and after the first wall was painted, a little paint ending up on the floor, it was easily apparent that the remaining paint was not sufficient for the rest of the walls. So, in the same way that she practiced ingenious cooking, Mother added an ingredient: some vaguely green paint she had used for lawn furniture a year or two ago. There was a little difference in the color of the paint, but perhaps it would not be noticed so much since we had stopped painting at the closet door and begun again on the other side.

An hour or two later, Donley lifted her three-inch brush from the coffee can she was using to hold her paint and offered the considered opinion that, once again, we were in trouble. Our walls were going to exceed our paint supply. We consulted with our maternal parent once more, and again, she found the solution on the old paint shelf in the cellar. A quart of white paint would surely eke out the supply and change the color only slightly. Unfortunately, the paints did not mix at all well and the quart of white paint lay sullenly in streaks all through the green paint can. At the end of the day when she mounted the stairs to pass judgment on the work we had accomplished, even Mother was astonished. She who rarely lost her composure over anything of as little importance as a painting job gulped and found nothing to say.

We had one mint green wall, two halves of bastard green walls, and the remaining walls seemed to be striped irregularly, something like the tigers one saw in the zoo, supposing they had eaten something that dared to disagree with them.

There was available back then, and perhaps still is if you know where to look, strips of wallpaper approximately two and a half inches wide that were used at the ceiling line, I suppose to highlight the paint job and hide uneven strokes as the ceiling line met the wall line.

In our sloping walled bedroom, they had the added advantage of acknowledging just what was considered ceiling and what was wall. We had a lot of that stuff, so Mother went back to her supply and chose one that was not only intended for use in a green room, but that was printed with jungle-type growth. It went very well with the room. There was enough there to outline the closet door and the door opening off the hall. We also placed a strip under each window. After we had scrubbed the bare wood floor and re-hung the curtains, cutting down on the light that poured in, especially at the south window, the paint job didn't look too bad, particularly if you squinted with the left eye and held the right one open very wide. It just looked as if strange shadows were being thrown up on the wall by firelight. It would have looked even more convincing if the room had boasted a fireplace.

We told Carrington to be sure to figure on enough paint. We wanted no repetition of the bedroom decorating. She rechecked her figures and doubled her original estimate from two gallons to four, pushing the price far beyond our budget. Luke took the paper in one hand and studied Carrie's figures. He was going to collect his paper route money on Saturday, and he would make up the difference between our available money and our needs. He said it in a throw-away manner that impresses me to this day, and when we all ooohed and aaahed at his generosity, he added his proviso. He, Luke, being the major stockholder in this bold plan, could not also be expected to take part in the actual work. Carrington found the piece of paper on which she had noted what tools we would need to get the work accomplished and crossed out the number five next to paint brushes and carefully re-entered a four.

It was hard getting all that paint home from the hardware store. I certainly had no idea how much a gallon of paint weighs. Carrington went after school on Tuesday and spent over an hour choosing the paint.

"I picked the warmest color they had in the store. I could tell by the name," she said proudly.

She took it immediately to her friend Suemarie, who lived two houses down from the store. On Thursday, she informed us, the four of us would have to go after school, pick it up, and carry it home, where it could be hidden in the barn until Mother and Pop left on Saturday. It was a good two miles from Suemarie's house to ours, and when we carried that paint three blocks, the palms of our hands were marked by red welts from the thin wire of the handle. I swear that my own arms grew approximately one and a half inches on the trip home, and Luke, in order to prove how tough he was, never switched his burden from hand to hand and to this day has one arm longer than the other. But then maybe he always did have that longer arm. We always said he was half gorilla, so maybe the right half was the gorilla half.

It was a good thing Carrie was so enthused over her idea, since the tide of her enthusiasm carried the rest of us. When I say my prayers nowadays, I pray for eternal happiness and bountiful blessings on the man who invented the paint roller. Would that he had been placed on this earth a generation earlier. Some days when time hangs heavily, I try to figure how many miles of three-inch brush strokes are required to cover an ordinary sized kitchen. Isn't there a device that measures the miles walked? Then surely it is only fair that you ought to be able to re-enact that day and measure the miles the arm went up and down, backwards, and forwards.

Opening the paint can was a shocker. Carrington kept secret the colors she had chosen, wanting to surprise us. She sure surprised me. The paint that looked pale pink when we opened the can, when stirred, brightened to a color that looked like somebody stirred too many strawberries into the ice cream.

"Hot pink!" Carrington crowed delightedly. "What could be warmer than hot pink?"

She reminded us of the conversation heard over the radio about warm colors. Made sense to me.

"And for the woodwork..." Carrie continued. Our kitchen boasted a waist-high wainscot where there weren't all those doors and it and the doors and windows had always been painted white or ivory. "For the woodwork," she repeated enthusiastically, raising a paint can over her head in triumph, "Chocolate brown!"

Luke moved the two paint colors closer and peered into the depth of the gallon cans. "You think they'll go good together?"

"They're warm colors," Carrington announced confidently, "and warm goes with warm."

By working hard all day with a brief stop for sandwiches and an even shorter supper break, we finished that day. With floor mopped, windows scrubbed clean of chocolate brown paint, and appliances washed off, we sat and waited for our mother to come home to her Mother's Day surprise.

She came in about nine o'clock. Any doubts we may have entertained about her being surprised were soon laid to rest. Anybody could have faked the gasp and the stagger as she viewed the re-decoration of the kitchen, but nobody can make the color drain from their face the way it happened to Mother then.

"Do you like it? It's a surprise for Mother's Day." In the flurry of questions that followed and the shrill explanation of the putative warmth that would derive all winter from our choice of colors, Mother had several minutes before she had to reply.

"It certainly is different," she said. While it wasn't quite as laudatory an answer as we expected, we were satisfied because we knew how pleased she must be. After all, any kid knows there's nothing as nice as a surprise.

In the week or so following, the time of daylight was stretching, and we rose in almost full daylight. I found myself, day after day, eating breakfast with my eyes closed as the morning light brightened the hot pink and illuminated the chocolate brown. Once when I opened my eyes to butter my toast, I noticed that most of the family was either closing their eyes over their breakfast or studiously casting their eyes downward at the plate.

Two days before school was out, we suffered an unfortunate grease fire in the kitchen. Mother fried a whole skilletful of chicken and put it in the refrigerator for supper. Forgetting the skillet, she had gone to take the garbage out. Coming back in, she found the kitchen door stuck and was unable to get in. Just as the skillet of grease burst into flames, Mother's frantic working of the kitchen door managed to free it, and she entered just in time to smother the flames with baking soda that happened to be standing nearby. The only damage was the smoke blackening the kitchen walls. They would have to be repainted.

It as almost like a judgment the way it worked out. For instance, Mother never, never took the garbage out. It was Trent's job, and Mother was religious about each person doing his own job. And the first time she broke her own rule, look what happened. It sure was a good thing supper was already prepared too, because Pop liked his meals on time and there was no way something could have been cooked after that mess.

When the insurance adjuster came to view the damage, he agreed to pay not only to have the walls repainted, but also for our labor to have them washed down first, and our time cleaning up the mess.

I was pretty happy about the idea of having our kitchen professionally painted, but my pleasure was dispelled quickly when Mother came home the day after she received the insurance check with gallons of white enamel and blue wall paint.

"The pink and brown were nice," she said , "But as long as we're painting, we might as well change the colors. And no use paying somebody else to do what we can do ourselves, especially with school out.

It took three coats to cover, light blue over hot pink and white over chocolate brown. Even Ragan didn't escape the arduous project. For three days she joined us, managing to do almost half as much as Carrie, who was used to work. I heard Ragan grumbling the first day and then grousing later about having to undo damage she hadn't been responsible for and then something about a dumb Mother's Day gift that hadn't been her idea in the first place. Just as if the lovely Mother's Day surprise had anything to do with the fire.

Mother heard her too, I guess, because she responded, fingering the dollars left over from the insurance check, that it was the best Mother's Day gift she ever received.

She used some of the settlement to buy a couple of new sweaters. All the old ones had to be thrown out because they were full of soot and smoke.

Chapter Fifteen

It never occurred to me to wonder why my parents had chosen each other to spend their lives with, 'till death did them part. Perhaps, probably, I never realized they made the choice. I assumed that God had ordained them to be my parents and as such, they sprang fully made and mated into being. In much the same way, he had ordained Donley to be my sister and best friend, and Trent and Luke to be brothers I would like and count on. Of course, one questions the wisdom of the Almighty in the case of Ragan and Vala. I think he made a mistake and got them into the wrong family. Or perhaps the mistake was made at the local hospital.

As far as I can recall, Ragan never got her hands dirty with housework. She would not have fed the chickens for any reason less than an act of God. She neither toiled nor did she spin, but unlike the lilies of the field, she ate, dressed well, and made her presence felt. Had needlework still been considered the appropriate pastime for ladies, she would have been right in there with the best of them, tiny-stitching away. As it was, she sang in the choir, danced in the chorus at school, and arranged flowers. At least she knew how, having taken a 4-H class

On a hot summer day, when Pop decreed that the sweet corn patch nearest the road needed to be hoed—"And I mean every single row"—before supper, we entreated Mother to make Ragan help, since there was an extra hoe. But Ragan was busy sewing buttons on a blouse she would need for school.

"It's a poor house that can't afford one lady," Mother told us. I was often sorry that I hadn't been born first so I could have taken the position. It was filled admirably by the time I came along. Only belatedly did it occur to me that in a house as large as ours, surely two ladies could be afforded, but by that time Vala had usurped the position of second lady right out from under my nose.

If there is something to reincarnation and a person has the opportunity to be reborn into a large family, the best position is either first or last. Second or second to last would be all right too. Or oldest daughter. As anyone in the civilized world would confirm, and I am not speaking here of sociologists but of members of large families, the very worst place to be born is right in the middle. It's hardly necessary to explain why. Everybody is excited about the first baby. The knowledge of the impending arrival is announced to grandparents as long as eight months before the expected moment. Little garments are made, blankets quilted, a crib prepared. Often, the second baby is greeted with only slightly less enthusiasm, particularly if he has the good judgment to wait a couple of years.

Only a true saint, of whom very few can be found on the family tree, can sustain undiminished enthusiasm beyond the fourth and fifth. By the time Luke, Trent, Donley, and I arrived, with less than four years between Luke and me, Mother was not precisely bored but jaded and exhausted by the experience.

Then the last one comes along. How can you be sure the last one is the last one? I don't know, but my folks apparently did. When Vala came upon the scene, there was a resurgence of enthusiasm that paled anything that had gone before. Her least accomplishment was greeted with handclapping and cries of wonder. Just for instance: say that I had memorized the entire list of popes of the Catholic Church—something which would have secured my position at the top of the class with the nuns for the rest of my life but something I never did actually accomplish. But say I did. Do you think Mother would have stopped the family from tucking into pork chops, chicken and dumplings, or meatloaf, while I entertained them with "Peter, Linus, Cletus, Clement" even for half the long, long list. Of course not. But when Vala sang an oft-repeated commercial and insisted on entertaining the supper table gathering with it, not a salt shaker was expected to move, regardless of the length of the song. Fortunately, there was never a sustained performance. How many choruses are there to the Campbell's soup song? She was kind of cute with her fuzzy halo of hair so fine she looked almost bald in the bright light, her big blue eyes, and her feed sack, cornflower spotted dress, swinging her high-topped white shoes against the slats of the high chair in time with her singing. I would have liked her better if she were not so obviously the pet.

I had the job of getting her dressed in the morning. Vala had what seemed to be a vast wardrobe, probably because everything that I, Donley, Carrington, and Ragan had ever owned was passed down, and she was the ultimate passee. Also her small size could be accommodated by one feed sack.

I didn't mind buttoning her into the pretty, printed dresses worn in the warm weather. It was the winter dressing I hated. The airy pinafore garments went right over her arms, buttoned in the back, and Bob's your uncle, the kid was ready to meet the world. Who needs shoes anyway when it's warm?

But when the frost was on the pumpkin, it was also in our house, and Vala had to be coaxed into an undershirt and shirt, flannel-lined corduroys, shoes, and matching socks. They didn't match her outfit; they matched each other. Two alike were hard to come by, and I didn't see why it mattered anyway, since her pants more than met her white-topped shoes, and who could see her doggoned socks anyway? But Mother insisted.

Vala was not imbued with a spirit of cooperation. She held her arms stiffly at her sides to make it more difficult for me to drag a garment over her, and she refused to lift a leg so I could slide her slacks on. Worst of all, when it came time to put her shoes on, she would double up her toes and swing the foot, sometimes delivering a sharp kick to my cheek, my forehead, or nose as I strove to capture the foot and force it into the imprisoning shoe.

"Help her?" I would say in despair. "I wouldn't mind helping her. I mind doing it against her will."

One day, frustrated beyond my ability to bear up, I bit her foot, and in her surprised pain, she undoubled her toes long enough for me to slide the shoe easily on, and from then on, I did not hesitate to use fear tactics.

My other form of retaliation was to choose the ugliest clothes in her closet and dress her in them. Of course, she always told, but I would disclaim innocently that I thought the plaid shirt looked very nice with the polka dot pants, and I'd perfected my innocent look so well that Mother never believed me guilty of anything but bad taste. And she was far too busy to undertake a change of clothing for Vala simply for reasons of vanity. Believe me, when the kid learned to dress herself, I led the cheering, and my folks said that at last I seemed to have learned to love my baby sister. I did learn to love her, but it was about the time they all quit calling me Digger. The nicest thing about being from a big family is that when you lose patience with one member or are temporarily holding one in dislike, there is always another to turn to.

There were too many years between me and my two oldest brothers for me to feel very close to them as a youngster, but I remember as a teenager I went to my very first major league ballgame, and it was my brother Conner who took me, Donley, and Trent. It was a two and a half hour drive, unless you kept the car in overdrive all the way, which Conner did. He was proud of himself because he passed every car on the road that day. His driving, then and now, is a testament to the infinite mercy of the Lord, who has allowed him to continue to live in spite of it.

It was a memorable day in our lives. The Cardinals of St. Louis made more runs that the opposition, crossing the plate eighteen times, while the New York Giants scored only four times. This is something the Cardinals have consistently failed to do, when as an adult, I go to see them play. But what I remember best was the layout of the field. We had played a lot of ball: softball—a treacherous name for a ball which can loosen half a dozen teeth without even trying, football, keep away…the list is endless. The major leagues had it all over us. Heck! Having uniforms is one thing, but the really big advantage they had was that they did not have to move off their playing field every time a car came along. I noticed that while there were only three bases (first, second, and third), there were four men to man them. Heavens! It hardly seemed fair to allot more than one man to each base. Someone kindly informed me that the fourth man was the shortstop. And I thought all the time that a shortstop was a swiftly turned play.

The thing that stymied me longest—indeed it was the fifth inning before enlightenment came—was the absence of the deep outfielder. I had been listening for years to the ball games and heard often that Stan Musial or Country Slaughter was playing "deep," and since "deep outfielder" had always been my position on the team, I had felt a thrill of something shared with the stars. Now I looked to see who was playing "deep outfielder," and it seemed to me, from my place in the stands, that all the outfielders were at about the same depth. I scanned the scorecard for a clue but in vain. It called out right, center, and left. No deep.

You don't have to hit me over the head with a bat for me to realize the score. I thought of how I could never hit the ball through the little wire things in croquet. I pondered on the ability of the ball to get through the little squares in my tennis racket, I recalled the times the football had come hurtling toward me in a perfect spiral, only to fall in the dust at my feet. I didn't even ask about deep outfielders.

I had the theory that Pop never really looked at us. I gathered evidence from day to day until I was convinced that my theory was irrefutable. How else could you explain the many, many times he called me Donley? Of course, a scant year's difference in age could have accounted for some of the confusion, but how about the times he called me Luke? Donley complained, as did Carrington, about his inability to address us by the correct names.

"If you don't know my name, my number is four," Carrington told him. He didn't remember that either, and went merrily along, calling off names, until somebody answered, and he knew he had the right kid.

"Luke," he said to me one day, when I was wearing overalls, "Go tell your mother that I'm going to the Sedley auction. See if she wants to go."

It must have been a farm auction since Pop wore his well-mended, less well-laundered work pants, and a shirt with a hole newly torn in it.

Mother had a cake in the oven, and I could see she was torn between her attempt to wrest a perfect baking from the coal oil range and an opportunity to go to the auction. Even as she was trying to make up her mind, she slipped into the bedroom behind the kitchen and was slipping off the kitchen-marked dress she was wearing, and slipping into something just as informal but clean. She emerged and announced, "I think I'll go with your father. Watch the cake."

Easy enough to say now, when ovens have little glass windows through which you can peek, venturing no greater damage than a scorched nose if you peered too closely. Mother had gone off without so much as telling me how many minutes the cake had been baking and how many remained before its completion. What to do? What to do?

I applied the smell test. Sniff, snoggle, I pulled as much air as I could through my nose, testing the atmosphere for cooking cake smells. My nose said coal oil. I found the downstairs book I was currently reading. I had long since learned that in order to save time and get through as many books as possible, it was better to have a book for downstairs and a book for upstairs. Then whenever providence allotted you a minute to read a page, you could take what time was offered without losing minutes scrabbling upstairs or downstairs to find reading matter. I read ten pages and nose-tested the atmosphere in the immediate vicinity of the oven again. My nose said mmmmm chocolate. Okay, that meant within ten minutes that cake was probably going to be ready for consumption. Given the kind of book I was reading, I figured a page and a half a minute, so I read fifteen more pages. Once more, I dragged a quart of air through my nostrils. This time my nose detected the smell of burning. I whipped open the oven door, and two things fell within my immediate range of vision. A small piece of last night's biscuit had fallen to the oven floor and lay in blackened misery, surrounded by a pool of grease that had once been in integral part of it. Worse, the chocolate cake was slowly but inevitably sinking, its peaked top, as if undercut by subterranean torments, collapsing into the bottom of the oblong pan.

I closed the oven door for a minute and thought. Carrington came to my rescue. She drew the cake out of the oven and told me not to turn it out onto a plate. We would just ice it in the pan.

"But Mother didn't say anything about icing it." I whined.

"She didn't say anything about making it fall by opening the door at just the wrong minute, did she," Carrington replied in her know-it-all fashion.

She brought down a large bowl and doubled all the ingredients for powdered sugar icing. She scrounged around in the cupboards until she found a double handful of raisins she could soften by stewing in water for a few minutes, some dried-out coconut, and half a package of nuts Mother had hidden so well that she'd forgotten them. It was a little like a landfill operation, dumping all that stuff into the crater in the middle of the cake. When we finished, the cake was as level as a golf course, even as the one-time dump becomes a park. There were places on that cake where the icing was as thick as your wrist, but only we who had iced it knew that.

When Mother arrived home, having acquired a ratty looking dresser, which, once cleaned up, would be ideal for the room Luke, Trent, and Martin shared, she was pleased at the way I had watched her cake, and I didn't say anything.

I went into the backyard with all the other kids to open the drawers of the dresser, to check if somebody had hidden and forgotten a shoe box full of cash, twenty carats of diamonds, or a letter with Abraham Lincoln's signature. Nobody had, which made it about the thirty-eighth time in the last twelve years that nobody had. I know. I checked every time Mother brought home another piece of auction sale furniture. But I'd keep looking.

If Mother was surprised when she cut into the cake to serve it for supper, she remained silent. I noticed that she was a little more discerning about what she served to whom. Trent and Luke each received a piece of icing lightly undercoated with cake. Pop got a piece from the middle: half cake, half landfill. He enjoyed it apparently, for he asked for seconds. When he finished the second piece, he looked at Donley.

"That was a very good cake, Vala."

I don't know whether he meant to congratulate me or Carrington.

Chapter Sixteen

Carrington was an inspired cook before she entered her teens. Her cakes were light and moist, her yeast rolls rivaling the best Mother produced. She was a godsend in a family like ours.

Mother guarded her preserved vegetables and fruits jealously. Months after the peas were gone from the garden, we could not open a jar of peas because carrots and tomatoes were still available. Mother did not consider variety in our meals to be of greater importance that fresh-from-the-garden taste. She allowed no one to open anything until the growing season was ended by the first killing frost. On canning days, I always hoped for the jar that didn't seal so I could have a taste of strawberry jam before the dead of winter. Even after winter fell, she was still cautious. No one could open a jar of cherries for pie unless she opened two jars and stretched them over three pies.

So rigid was her rule of using garden produce when it was available that on one occasion when she was making spaghetti sauce, she asked Vala to get her some tomatoes. Vala was not used to being sent on errands, but she departed cheerfully enough. Mother waited and waited and waited. Finally she removed her ground meat from the heat and went to look for Vala. She found her bending over the hot bed looking for the best tomato plants to pull. One or two were already lying on the ground beside her.

"But you said never to use a vegetable from the cellar when it's growing outside," Vala explained plaintively.

Sometimes when March drew to a close and the tractor was being tuned up for spring plowing and planting, Mother would survey her remaining stores—the golden peaches, the ruby tomatoes in their glass jars now overlaid with a light dust—and realize that she would need those jars empty before long. Then we ate very well for three months, three or four different vegetables finding their concurrent way to the dinner table.

In Carrington's case, the rules were suspended. Did Carrington want to open a jar of plums to try a new dish? Her decision was applauded. Perhaps Carrie wanted to experiment with a casserole that called for three different vegetables. Mother would dig out the turkey roaster and encourage her to carry on.

When it was time for walnuts, we went to the publicly owned land around the lake to gather the fallen fruit, each nut in its green hull, as big around as a slightly shrunken tennis ball. Baskets and baskets of the nuts were carried home to be laid out in the hayloft to dry so the hulls could be removed. For days after a hulling session, we went around with hands stained brown from the juice of the hulls.

"Yah!" Trent would lift brown hands on freckled arms in front of Vala's face, sending her screaming to Mother.

With nuts too, Mother was profligate at Carrie's request.

"I'm making fudge," Carrington would announce in the middle of a Sunday afternoon. "I'll need some nuts."

Mother would nod. Yes, Carrie could use fifteen nuts, and the boys would shell them for her.

"That's not enough," Carrie replied, "I'm making a double batch, and I don't like to stint on nuts."

Carrie would take Mother's assent for granted and count out twenty-five nuts, which the boys shelled eagerly because they liked fudge. Of course, Mother must have enjoyed a sweet tooth too or she might have objected.

Close to Christmas, when Mother began assembling the things she would need to make her famous fruitcake—a dark, rich recipe of dough, nuts, and raisins that is lost forever in the mists of time—Carrie suggested that they make candy as well. The little fruitcakes were intended for gifts, and perhaps some of the people on the gift list would prefer candy one year instead. They probably would have been more appreciative of receiving both, but our gifts did not run to quite that much.

Carrie borrowed a marble candy slab from Suemarie. I don't know if it was their proximity to the hardware store or what, but that family had every gadget devised by man. Caramels were a natural; we had our own cream and butter and even nuts, so it was sort of a free gift. They must have made twenty-five pounds, allowing the rest of us gathered hungrily around the manufacturing operation to sample a piece now and then usually a piece from an uneven end. Once we had it in our mouths, it made little difference. Then Carrington branched out into peanut brittle. We didn't get many tastes of that, partly because peanut brittle is just that: brittle. All the pieces were irregular and who could tell if a piece was broken? Besides that, we had to buy the peanuts.

It took only the little taste I had to convince me that Carrington had done extremely well. Sometimes I worried that some talent scout of cookery would discover Carrington and snap her up to work for someone else and the rest of us would starve to death. I could picture her in a high, white chef's hat with lesser mortals running around, just as Donley and I did.

"Little girls!" Carrie was barely five years older than I, four years older than Donley. "Get down here and get the potatoes peeled."

It wouldn't be hard for Carrie to make the adjustment from Moss-ive kitchen to massive kitchen.

We hoped that the boxes of peanut brittle would outnumber the prospective recipients so that we could spirit away some of the candy and eat it, but no such luck. When the list was made and there proved to be two boxes left over, Mother promptly added the sisters from St. Albert's to her gift list. We grumbled, and Trent hissed, "Those nuns are fat enough."

On the first day of Christmas vacation, Mother and Aunt Petty always joined a couple of old friends in an all-day shopping trip. Not that either Mother or Aunt Petty bought much. They had long since stitched, baked, knitted, or bought on sale all the Christmas presents. Indeed, Aunt Petty had been known to make a Christmas dress for one child and when Christmas drew near, gift it to another child since the first child had grown more than had been allowed for the previous April or May. Mother and Aunt Petty just enjoyed the crowds, the dime store Santa Clauses, and the shops trimmed for Christmas. Keep in mind that back then, stores were not decorated for Christmas on the day after Halloween, so when Mother and her sister went out to look late in December, the decorations were still fresh, not shop-worn.

Later they would come back to one house or the other for a festive lunch, and this year it was Mother's turn to entertain. Besides the usual four people, there would be one extra: Mother's cousin Louellen. She was visiting some of her family. Had it been the four old friends alone, little sandwiches would have been plenty elegant enough, but since Louellen would be here, Mother found it necessary to outdo herself. For some reason, Louellen always brought out the worst in Mother and forced her to bring out the best in herself. That sounds a little complicated, but the reality was that Mother was beautifully spoken, as well dressed as she could manage, and the food was far above average and impeccably served when Sort-of-Aunt Louellen came. And for all the worst possible reasons.

Today Mother asked Carrie to make dainty little morsels of food that delighted the eye but had to be consumed in extravagant numbers to fill the stomach. Everything stood ready in the refrigerator or on the shelves of the enclosed back porch when Aunt Petty picked Mother up. She advised us sternly not to touch a thing until she returned home, though we should set the table for lunch and use the good china, which meant no chipped glasses and no cracked plates.

For once, Donley and I were on our own. Ragan had taken Vala and Martin on the bus to have their picture taken with Santa. For some reason, Vala and Martin were exhorted to believe in the jolly old elf. This was a change from several years ago, when Mother and Pop decried the myth. It cost too much to provide Christmas presents for all of us for them to want to share the credit with some fat, red-suited myth. Perhaps we were a little more prosperous by then and Mother and Pop were not struggling so hard to provide Christmas gifts, so didn't mind so much sharing the credit with Mr. Claus. Both Carter and Conner were away, home hopefully for Christmas Day, but no longer than that. Luke and Trent had seasonal jobs, and Carrie had gone to the high school to help with preparations for the Glee Club's choral symphony later in the week.

It felt funny to be in the house all by ourselves. At our grown-up ages of barely teen and barely pre-teen, it seldom happened, and the feeling of freedom was heady. We spent a few minutes admiring the Christmas tree. We pulled the drapes to darken the living room and turned the tree lights on—the better to appreciate the little colors shining so brightly. But then they all went out, as series lights were wont to do, and we spent a good twenty minutes looking for the one bad bulb that caused the entire string of lights to fail and gave up. We unplugged the lights, leaving it for somebody else to discover that the lights weren't working and why.

We opened the drapes and felt all the Christmas presents piled under the tree—gifts exchanged between the ten of us. We drew names twice so everybody got two gifts from their brothers and sisters, but we had long since figured out what we were getting. I was getting ice skates from Carter and Vala. They were wrapped in two different packages in order to follow the rules of two packages per sibling and also to fool me. I was very pleased and had checked the creek every day to be sure it was frozen hard. Donley was getting an expensive fountain pen from Trent, which she had coveted, and mittens and matching hat from Martin. Mother did Martin's shopping and knitted both. Donley was less pleased about the hat and gloves than the pen.

Given our pre-knowledge, the presents lost their appeal very shortly, and we moved on out to the piano and treated ourselves to a self-performed concert of Christmas songs. That also palled soon because the music room had formerly been the side porch, and in the winter it still felt like a porch. It was cold. Inevitably, we were drawn to the goodies stored in the cool of the back porch. If you are very, very careful, you can lift icing off spots on cupcakes that are more heavily iced than they need to be and never be noticed. We did that for a while, but our appetite for sweets was tempted beyond our ability to pick off icing discreetly.

It was Donley's idea to make peanut brittle, not mine. She knew where Mother had hidden the peanuts left over from the earlier batch. There were leftovers of the other ingredients, too. She soon had them rounded up and laid out on the stove. She was rooting around in the cupboard looking for the same pan Carrie used when I remembered the marble slab. Carrie had imprudently and thoughtlessly returned it to its rightful owner without regard for her younger sisters' pleasure. How could we make candy without it?

"It doesn't matter," Donley said, acting as if she'd been making candy for years. She might have been chief tester in the laboratories of Fannie Mae, for all the worry the lack of a mere marble slab caused her. "We can pour it on the table. The top is slick as marble." She wiped her hand across the gray, plastic top to prove it.

"But it's not the same!"

"Do you think the candy will notice?" Donley snorted, disdainful of my carping at trifles, and got on with measuring out sugar and salt into the pan. We had never heard of a candy thermometer, but we dropped bubbling syrup into cold water until a ball formed. That was the way Carrie tested her Sunday fudge and it worked okay for peanut brittle too.

"You forgot to butter the table," Donley cried, and reached for the bowl of butter from the fridge. With her free hand, she slathered the middle of the table with butter while I stood back and tried to remember whether Carrington had buttered the marble slab. I didn't think she had.

The liquid pouring out of the heavy pan was lovely, a dark amber, and I licked my mental chops in anticipation of the candy we would be eating shortly. I didn't worry what Mother would say when she found her store of hidden peanuts gone. Sufficient unto the day had always been my motto.

Donley was back in the cupboard searching for the one pound coffee tins my mother collected from friends and relatives all year. If one was good enough to send our Christmas gifts in, it was plenty good enough for Donley and me to horde our goodies in. The peanut brittle glistened wetly on the table but just at the edge, surely it was beginning to harden a little.

I put out a tentative finger to test. I had no nails to slide beneath the surface of the puddle of candy and with my finger, couldn't seem to move the edge of the peanut brittle. Perhaps with a knife.

"Donley, I can't budge this peanut brittle." I know my voice sounded like an announcement of doom, but even with a knife, I was unable to pry the slightest piece of peanut brittle from the buttered tabletop. Furthermore, I couldn't slide the knife beneath the hardening mound in order to pry it up. That peanut brittle and that tabletop had formed an unbreakable alliance.

Donley was airy. "Let me see, Digger. You must be doing something wrong."

A small wrinkle of worry marred her smooth blond brow as she reached into the drawer for something less flexible, but narrower, than the table knife. She brought out the honed-to-an-invisible-point knife Pop used to skin rabbits or slice slab bacon. She succeeded only in scratching the table's surface and cutting her own thumb. "Digger, it's stuck."

Holy cats! I could see that for myself. Now what were we going to do about it?

"Digger," said Donley, "What are we going to do about it?"

No help from that direction, I could see. It was I who suggested the hammer, and we used it with reckless abandon and managed to chip off an infinitesimal amount of the something-less-than-brittle candy. Then all at once, we managed to get off half a dozen pieces bigger than a silver dollar. We ate them while we deliberated on our next step.

Donley glanced at the clock.

"Digger, Mother will be home in an hour and a half, and she's planning to have a fancy lunch party at this table."

I knew that too, for cat's sake. Why didn't Donley help matters by telling me something I didn't know? Like whether we could get this stuff off the table, or if our only course of action was packing our bags and running away.

Poor Donley! She went hysterical when things went badly wrong, and this was about as wrong as things could get. Now my sister was laughing so hard that I thought her face was turning blue.

"I guess this means we won't have to use the good china," she gasped around her wheezing laughter. "Everybody can just lick dessert off the table."

I started laughing, too. I could just see Sort-of-Aunt Louellen sticking out her sharp tongue while bent from the waist and straightening up to say, "Darling, how really truly unique." But all that laughing wasn't getting that tabletop clean.

"I always said we should never have turned the dining room into a bedroom for the boys," Donley giggled. I didn't immediately follow Donley's reasoning. "If we had a dining room, we could set the table in there."

Donley was working with a chisel now, but to little avail. Every time a chip of any size flew off the mass, we paused long enough in our chipping to find and eat it.

We tried everything we could think of. We used very hot water poured directly on the mess with no luck. We began to think of it more as a burden than as a treat, willing to sacrifice the whole week of crunching peanut brittle in the dark quiet of our midnight bedroom for a solution to our ever closer problem.

We plugged in the heating pad and turned it to high to try to soften the rock hard surface, but with no better success than the water. We tried household cleansers, and by this time we would never have been able to eat that candy with the best will in the world. Absolutely nothing worked or at least worked well enough. Not the scouring pads, not the scrub brush. We thought about having the dog in to see if he could lick the table clean, but when he was coaxed up onto the table, the smell of bleach put him off.

We were looking at the clock again and estimating the length of time we had left until the grownups arrived and also the time we had left to live. There was no doubt in our minds that our mother would kill us when Louellen saw our kitchen table caught in a vise of peanut brittle. Suddenly, we heard a knock at the door. We looked at each other and silently debated the wisdom of seeking refuge under the bed, but of course Mother wouldn't have knocked. Perhaps that knock was salvation.

In a way it was. Aunt Petty stood on the front porch with the two old friends of her youth, Mrs. Alcott and Mrs. Ranger. All three were smiling, still full of the fun they had been having downtown and pleased with their morning's accomplishments. Caught. We were solidly and surely caught, and there was nothing left but to throw ourselves on the mercy of our aunt, which Donley promptly did.

"Oh, Aunt Petty, we only meant to surprise you all with a lovely gift and it's all gone wrong."

Not one word about the plans for pigging up the peanut brittle ourselves under cover of night so we didn't have to share with Vala. Donley began to sob, very realistically, and I stood open-mouthed and gazed in awe at her until I remembered that I had better start sobbing too. I wasn't nearly as proficient.

We were too involved with our sobbing to tell Aunt Petty the cause of our pseudo anguish, so she headed for the kitchen. Aunt Petty had enough children and experience to know that the heart of many a disaster lies in the kitchen. We heard her laughing almost as hard as Donley had done earlier, but she was more resourceful.

"Quick, girls. Your mother stayed a few minutes with Louellen to chat with old Mrs. Wabner, but she'll be along in a few minutes. Bring me a sheet and your mother's best tablecloth."

Aunt Petty was a quick thinker. Within minutes, she had dispatched Donley to the barn for a small flat basket the peaches came in last summer. She found Pop's sharp knife where Donley and I left it lying out and with it cut out as much of the bottom of the basket as necessary so the rim fit around the circumference of the peanut brittle. With the table covered, the sheet between the gooey mess and the good cloth, and the basket set down on the whole thing, it was hard to see that the surface of the table was a series of carbuncle-like ripples and bumps within the circumference of the basket. Mrs. Alcott and Mrs. Ranger went outside in their good coats to cut green branches off the pine tree behind the barn and pick as many pinecones as they could find in the light covering of snow. Aunt Petty divested all their packages of the bright ribbons, and with a few walnuts and three of the shiniest red ornaments off the Christmas tree, created a centerpiece which looked…well, it looked lots better than a glob of amber goo in the middle of the table.

If Mother was surprised when she showed up with Louellen very shortly thereafter, she didn't show it. Perhaps she had been expecting us to put together a centerpiece.

Donley and I didn't forget for a minute what was hidden under that basket of greenery. We were so polite every minute that had Mother been paying attention, she would have rushed us off to bed with a thermometer in our collective mouth before you could say sticky, chewy peanut brittle. We passed the little things that had been prepared, we took only the smallest helpings on our plates, and politely refused seconds. We poured coffee and tea cheerfully and in general impressed Sort-of-Aunt Louellen, who remembered us dimly as a couple of ruffian-like tomboys she would never encourage her own daughters to associate with.

If anyone's behavior left something to be desired, it was Mrs. Ranger's. She made heavy use of her lacy handkerchief all through the meal to cover something that was supposed to be a sneeze or a cough but sounded like a snort of laughter to me. By the time the last drop of coffee drained from the last dainty china cup, her complexion was as bright as the ornaments in the peach basket. When Louellen took her leave, Mrs. Ranger did not join the other ladies in walking her to the door. She stayed right where she was and laid her head down on the table and, as my brothers would say, laughed her ass off. When Mother, Aunt Petty, and Mrs. Alcott came back from bidding farewell to the fifth member of their little shopping expedition, she sat up and wiped her eyes and told us to pass the goodies again. She hadn't been able to enjoy a single bite, what with not being able to laugh at what they had put over on Louellen.

So Mother finally saw what had motivated the centerpiece on the kitchen table, and she was at least restrained in front of company. We left the centerpiece on the table during family supper that night, but afterward Mom removed the tablecloth and pried the white sheet off, leaving the peanut brittle covered with a white fuzz of lint.

"Better get to bed early girls," Mother said, without a trace of Christmas joy in her voice, "because in the morning you will be up good and early to clean this goop off the table." She held up a hand to halt the question that hovered on both our lips. "I don't know how you'll get it off, but you will get it off." She could be very mean.

That night, good old Trent failed to bank the furnace fire properly and about two in the morning it went out. The temperature dipped below zero, and Donley and I, awakened by our tired old alarm clock, crept down to a cold kitchen where the ice froze in a glass of water left out. The temperature outside the refrigerator was colder than the temperature inside, so the refrigerator had defrosted itself and a thin skim of ice lay on the floor where the ice had melted and refrozen. We rubbed our hands together and turned our attention to the kitchen table and the job that awaited us.

The peanut brittle was broken into chunks, and long fissures appeared in the surface through which you could see the color of the tabletop. We touched one chunk and the solid cake of confection moved. Somehow the cold loosened the peanut brittle from its death grip on the tabletop. And to think I had not believed in the good fairies before now.

In awed and grateful silence, we picked up the remains of yesterday's experiment in culinary art and piled it in the sink. We ran the water for a long time over the bits and pieces before we picked them out and lay them on a plate to dry. We washed and dried the spot on the table we had expected never to see again and, taking our plate of peanut brittle, we crept back to bed and warmth.

We gave the peanut brittle to our brothers, and they all said it was some of the best they had ever tasted. We never told them that the dog had turned up his nose at it.

Chapter Seventeen

Everybody else at school was glad to see spring come. Not me. I liked the snow. I liked to wrap my covers around me in the chill of my bedroom and reach a hand out into the frosty air to turn a page as I read. I liked to slide around on the frozen pond and slide down the near vertical slopes of the same pond on a sled.

Once I remember Conner took a slope too fast on his toboggan and caromed off into a cornfield where the stalks still stood. One stalk plunged into his cheekbone, fractionally missing his eye. He was rushed bleeding and frightened into the doctor's office, where stitches were taken and the doctor warned of an impending black eye. The bandage was so large and so awkwardly placed that the doctor ended up covering the entire eye.

"And Jane," he warned Mother, "don't let him read anything one-eyed."

The doctor knew us well enough to know which of us was most likely to have a nose buried in a book. Up until then, Conner had taken his injury lightly, but when he arrived home and found that he would not be able to read so much as the Sunday funnies, he very nearly wept. But that was a happenstance in a million. What is the statistical likelihood that you will get your eye damaged by a corn stalk while sledding downhill? And with Conner already having sustained such an injury, the probabilities of a recurrent incident were astronomical. So I took up my sled and flew down the hills again and again.

I liked tromping through the snow, provided that my boots were watertight. I liked building snow forts and pelting the rare passerby with snowballs. I liked the fire burning in the heating stove in the kitchen. I didn't like onion sets.

Half the student population at St. Albert's thought the robin was the harbinger of spring. The rest of us lived on acreage that was commonly called market gardens. We knew that before the robin had made it halfway back from Florida, our pops would be poring over order forms from the seed companies and determining how much ground should be allotted to green onions. The answer remained the same year after year. Too much.

The onion sets arrived in orange-colored net sacks, not heavy enough to be called burlap. Whey they lay out in the barn, I knew spring had arrived with the birds and the flowers and the mud on the street that made the nuns check our shoes as we came walking up each day, to gauge the damage to their clean floors. Our road was only truly hard-surfaced twice a year: once when the July sun baked it to a cement playing field and then when the temperature dropped way below freezing and left every rut and ridge diamond sparkling and diamond hard.

On a Friday in mid-April, I made my way home slowly, my heart as heavy as the bags of onion sets awaiting me. Onion sets are planted less than an inch apart and are set into the ground manually. Nobody but a man with lots of kids or lots of time would even consider planting green onions for obvious reasons. Take your average field, which is about five hundred feet long when planted in tomatoes. Now figure out if that field is twenty-seven rows wide, how many onion sets you would have to set an inch apart to have the field fully planted. Then consider the fact that any given field, when given over to onions, automatically grows at least twenty-five percent bigger. It's easy to see why I wasn't all that lyrical about the approach of spring.

All the way home I trudged, the rate of my progress matched only by crippled snails, Trent, Luke, Carrington, and Donley. But you can spend only so long gauging the depth of mud puddles along the route, admiring the rainbow colors made by motor oil dripped into a glassy puddle, and searching the murky depths of your soul to see if it would be a far, far better thing to do to run away.

"I want those three sacks planted before supper, Trent," my pop said, looking right at Luke.

We knew that he knew we had been dragging our homeward-bound feet. It started to drizzle before we even made it out to the field, our pans held out like beggar children seeking alms, so that Pop could pour an allotment of onions into them.

"You could have had these planted if you had hurried home the way I told you to do."

No sympathy and no use expecting it. There was nothing better for newly planted onions than a fine rain.

We planted and planted and planted. My fingernails were thick with rich dark mud, and my knees slid along frictionlessly through the damp field. I must have planted a billion of the little tiny things. At first, I planted them with a vengeance, thrusting each of the offensive buds into the ground as if I would bury it. But that was harder on me than it was on them, and I soon resorted to less energy-wasting methods.

"You're planting those onion sets upside down, Digger."

I looked up at Trent, who had been standing over me watching, just as if somebody had put him in charge of this operation.

"I'm not planting upside down," I said pleasantly and slid my muddy knee right into him, bowling him over.

"You are, too." He didn't stay down long and in coming up, he grabbed a clod of dirt and ground it into my hair.

"This is the way I've always planted onion sets, and I'm going to go right on planting onion sets this way until we are finished forever."

I was pretty mad by now, and Donley and Luke came back a few feet to see what Trent and I were yelling about.

"She's planting her onions upside down."

Boy, that Trent had a one-track mind.

"That's the way I plant mine," and Donley reached down and inserted an onion the same way I had been doing it to show the boys that it was my way and, incidentally, her way that was the approved, accepted method of planting onions.

"That's wrong, Donley." Trust Luke to side with Trent. "You're both planting your onions upside down."

I was ready to plant Luke and Trent upside down. Somebody called Carrington over, as if it were a matter where majority ruled. Carrington looked tired, her thin face was streaked with mud, her fingernails every bit as grungy as my own.

"I don't care if it's the right way or the wrong way. I have about a ton of homework to do so let's get the darned things planted."

We set to with a will, but looking over surreptitiously, I noted that Trent and Luke actually were putting their onions in exactly the opposite way that Donley and I were doing it. I wondered if I should change over, but decided that to do so would only be seen as an admission of error. I would have rather planted the entire field backwards than let the boys think they were smarter than I was.

We came to the end of a row and surveyed the number of onion sets left to plant. I had less than fifty; Donley had about the same. Carrington had about a thousand. Trent had only eight; he counted. Luke had slightly more than Donley and I, but he threw several dozen away, saying they looked rotten to him. Donley said onions all looked rotten to her. Could we throw the whole lot away? Speculation was born in Carrington's eyes, and she muttered about how cold it was becoming and wondered if onions planted in such damp, cold weather had any chance of coming up anyway. She mentioned how she would like to get in for supper, and where was Ragan anyhow, and when she had been Martin's age, she had been expected to help plant onions. After all, it didn't take any strength, just enough sense to know which side was up, a matter that perhaps shouldn't be discussed in view of our earlier disagreement, and finally, why didn't we just dig a hole over there under the apple tree that grew in the middle of this particular field and just dump the onion sets in?

Very seldom in the annals of civilization has such quick, complete agreement ever been reached unanimously. Within minutes, we were headed through the gathering darkness to the lights and warmth of the house with the buried, disposed-of onions setting as lightly on our consciences as we hoped Mother's hot biscuits would soon be setting on our digestive systems.

Nature abhors vacuums, leftovers, and kids who try to shirk their assigned tasks. Three weeks later, Pop went out to the field to pull up the first of the onion shoots, so tender a green, so tasty a morsel, only to find that every other row seemed to have grown much more than the alternate rows. He discovered the reason the minute he tried to pull up onions from two adjacent rows. In the second row, the onion had begun its growth downward from having been put into the ground root-side to the heavens. It made for a peculiarly shaped onion. Fortunately, there was a shortage of green onions on the market that year, so Pop was able to interest the grocery stores in his unusual shaped onions, which must have been a welcome diversion on many a relish tray all over the city that year. If he had not been able to market them, we would have had to eat a great many more green onions than anyone really wants to, because even our Mother and Aunt Petty together had never found a really good way to can onions.

Within another day or two, we faced the thundercloud of Pop's disapproval again. That's how long it took for the clump of onions we had thought disposed of to find its way into the light of the golden sunshine. Well, they had started further down into the bowels of the earth than the upside-down onions had. We buried them no less than a foot deep and never expected to see them again. I guess we should have known better. I've always suspected that onion plants are actively malevolent.

"What are these onions doing here?" Pop didn't even bother with a name, but we knew he was addressing the five of us.

"Looks like they seeded themselves there, and something in the soil must be really good for them," said Luke. He studied them carefully and nudged the uppermost growth with a toe. "Better not eat them," he said judicially. "They might be poisonous. Like mushrooms and other wild growing things."

"I'll just get the garden fork," Trent offered helpfully, "and turn them over so the little kids don't get sick or something."

Pop didn't quite believe it, but neither did he quite disbelieve either. He did not have all his troubles to look for.

Chapter Eighteen

My formal education consisted of eight grades at St Albert's, followed by four more at Mater Dei. I learned a lot at school. The first thing I learned was that while school might be dull compared to summer vacations, it sure beat staying home while Donley, Luke, and Trent went off for the whole day.

I also learned the easy way of multiplying or dividing by ten and how to find out if a multi-numeral number is divisible by nine or three. But I'm not telling here how it's done. This isn't any arithmetic book. I learned the principle exports of Argentina and promptly forgot them as soon as the test on the chapter was finished. I learned what Mater Dei meant. I learned how to forge the high school principal's name to an excuse so that neither I nor my best friends ever had to serve detention. It was good that we graduated when we did. They were beginning to get suspicious.

I learned that nobody else in the entire English-speaking world except the Moss family ate mayonnaise on their spinach. It was brought home to me one day at the age of fifteen in the cafeteria at Mater Dei, when for the first time spinach was served. "Yuck!" was the general consensus of opinion, but I liked spinach.

"Where's the mayonnaise for my spinach?" I asked the woman serving in the cafeteria.

Eight or nine kids down the line, I heard a noise like somebody was sick to the stomach, but I didn't connect it with my entirely reasonable request. Who ever heard of eating spinach, or asparagus for that matter, without a generous dob of mayonnaise? Apparently everybody except me and my pop, who insisted to the end of his life that the mayonnaise jar accompany any serving of those two vegetables.

Still, there were several things they never taught me at school. How to read, for instance, because I already knew how by the time I passed through those portals. Something else I learned: portals is derived from the Latin root word porto, meaning gate. When Donley entered first grade a year before me, she came home every afternoon bursting with knowledge and looking for someone to impress. I was impressionable. Donley got out her first grade reader, its cover darkened with myriad trips home through the rain and snow, with pages dog-eared but illustrations still bright, and she showed me how to make the letters that spelled out Dick and Jane; from then on, it was watch out, library. When I, myself, went to first grade, Sister Loretta Louise was astonished at how swiftly I mastered the reading books. I can hear her now saying to Sister Seraphica, "If only I knew how I taught her so easily, I could get it across to everybody."

Something else they never taught me at school was how to drive. There are some, I know, who say nobody ever taught me, that I never learned, but of course that's a lot of sour grapes. I drive with panache and flair, and my detractors suffer with envy.

There were no formal driver's education classes when I went to Mater Dei. Perhaps they wanted to include it in the curriculum, but nuns are by nature and by habit notoriously poor drivers, so perhaps the high school board in its infinite wisdom dissuaded them.

I learned to drive at home in the field with an International pickup as the student-training vehicle. All through our fifteen acres, paths wove between tomatoes and corn, green beans, and beets because otherwise it would have been a long haul up to the house with every bushel of produce. Sometimes when the snow was clean and everybody's enthusiasm for it was at a peak, Pop would attach the sled behind the tractor and pull us up and down those one-car-wide tracks.

I was fourteen the summer I decided I had been passenger long enough. Which meant Donley was fifteen, Trenton sixteen, and Luke seventeen. Both the boys had drivers licenses and considered that the driving chores were a male prerogative. Male chauvinists were thick on the ground back then; we just hadn't identified them yet. But one bright summer day, Luke went off to inquire about a job he'd heard of, and with the ratio of male to female halved,

Trent alone could not withstand the pressure. He let us take a turn at the wheel.

By the time Luke returned next day, convinced that it was a matter of staying near the phone to take the incoming call that would hire him, Donley and I had taken over. Trent thought we ought to use the clutch occasionally, but I saw nothing wrong with driving in first gear. It took us where we wanted to go. What I wanted to know how to do was steer. The niceties of fine driving could be left for later, and Trent took to walking back to the house a lot.

Luke stayed inside for two days, hovering around the telephone, getting upset when it was used. Since telephones were intended to be used, and since telephoning was Mother's favorite pastime, she was irritable but doing her best to cooperate. On the third day, she drove poor Luke out of the house, promising to call him with the dinner bell should the call come through. She promised on her word of honor to stay off the phone. Sure enough, that afternoon the dinner bell we hadn't heard for over a year rang across the tomato patch, calling Luke.

He jumped for the truck to find Donley firmly seated behind the wheel, ready at a word to chauffeur him to where duty called. We all piled in, front and back. If Luke was to have his fate decided, then his three nearest and dearest should be with him at the time. We raced as fast as first gear would carry us back to the house, where the three of us waited in the truck for Luke to come out.

He was beaming. Where lines of worry creased his forehead for the last three days, it was as if the sun had come forth over the face of the land. They wanted him. Well, we'd known that. Who wouldn't snap our brother up, given an opportunity? He was to go to Mendenhall tomorrow for a final interview and had already asked Mom to see whether his best shirt was in condition for such an interview or if it might need laundering. He needed to ask Pop for the loan of the car. He figured it all out and told us his plan as we stooped over the rows of tomatoes, divesting them of those ripe enough for market.

He would arise early in the morning, early enough to take Pop to work. Pop worked in a factory; the market garden, the pigs, the three cows, and the chickens were a sideline that he expected his children to take the largest burden of in order to support us. Then he would come home again to dress carefully, off to Mendenhall—an hour's drive—for the interview, and then home again in time to pick Pop up at work.

He wouldn't, of course, have to work in Mendenhall. That was the home office of the small chain of newspapers for whom he had been a carrier for these many years. Luke talked more that day than he had for the entire previous month. The underlying theme to his conversation was the absolute necessity of having the car on the morrow.

We had that field picked in record time, and the bushels of fruit loaded onto the back of the truck left no room for passengers until the tailgate was lowered.

"My turn to drive!" I said, taking advantage of Luke's euphoria to demand the position behind the wheel. I threaded my way cautiously through the fields and parked the truck, as was my custom, just one hundred feet short of the barn.

"Take it all the way in, Digger. I don't want to lug all those baskets all the way to the barn from here," Trent told me.

I didn't want to. The reason I generally parked where I had was the mulberry tree at the turn in the path. The mulberry guarded one side of the path, while a stout fence enclosing chickens stood a bare ninety inches away at the other side. I didn't feel competent enough to drive through there.

"Go ahead, Digger." said Trent.

I was too cowardly to say I didn't dare, so I did. Either that mulberry had grown a lot since yesterday or the load on the truck made it that much wider. As I made the turn at approximately one-half mile an hour, there was a scrunching sound, no louder than the noise you make opening a jar of peaches. *Grmmmp*, it said, just like the air entering the vacuum of the fruit jar. I knew I should have parked where I usually did.

We all climbed slowly out of the truck. Sure enough, the vehicle met the tree, and the tree got the better of it. Luke looked at me, looked at the dent in the fender, and shook his head. I think he would have left me to my just desserts, but he remembered the necessity of Pop being in a good mood for the furtherance of Luke's plans. When Pop's wrath descended, it landed on the just and the unjust, guilty and innocent, truck-denters and innocent passengers. Luke thought about it for a little while, and then he outlined his plan.

First, the truck was moved away from the tree, not by me. It was the work of a moment to dab enough mud on the old tree to hide the new wound in its bark. Then the truck was driven to the barn, again not by me, and its load removed from it to the sorting tables. Maneuvering back and forth, Luke managed to place the truck with its new dent directly beneath a storage shelf Pop had put up three years ago. On the storage shelf were various heavy objects, including a small sledge hammer. Luke removed all those items and then by pulling on the corner of the shelf, with Trent hanging onto him at the waist, they pulled that shelf down.

While Trent went off to find a small jar of vehicle paint that had come with the truck, we all arranged the items from the storage shelf casually around the truck, leaving a gasoline can lying on the fender. All the items, that is, except the sledge hammer. That we dabbed artistically with a bit of the paint Trent had found and left it in a direct line between where the shelf had been and the dent was now.

The plan was an example of genius at work. If the hammer had fallen from the shelf, somebody would have been in big trouble, and as I have said, when there was trouble for somebody, read everybody. But with the shelf having torn loose from its moorings, there was nobody to blame except the shelf builder, and we all know who that was.

Pop puzzled for a long time over what might have happened. The dent in the truck loomed of little account in his mind compared to the failure of a shelf he had thought would last nearly forever. Well, of course, Mother said, that garage was old and probably the rotting wood wasn't strong enough to hold the nails that Pop had used when he installed the shelf. He was simply too good a craftsman to be forced to work with inferior materials. This was reasoning Pop could live with, and the matter was forgotten. Pop used a little filler on the dent, asked if anyone had seen his little jar of paint, and was uncommonly pleased when Trent was able to put his hand on it at once. The filler and the improvised repair lasted as long as the truck did.

Luke went off to Mendenhall for his interview and landed the job. He hated it, and when he reached eighteen, gave it up to join the Navy.

I swore off driving for a good ten years, and after cursory practice, went down to take the driving test, eight months pregnant with my second child. Whether from compassion for a lady who badly needed to be able to drive or from fear that I would return the next day, the testing officer passed me with the warning that I should get a little practice before I drove out in heavy traffic. I didn't quite have enough courage to ask Pop if I could come over and get the practice in the field.

Chapter Nineteen

On a day in June, I went to work as usual, catching the bus with Donley, who worked for the same company as I did. More properly, I worked for the same company Donley worked for, and her presence there hadn't hurt my own chances for employment one whit. If Donley minded having a younger sister tagging after her into grade school, into high school, and into employment, she never said so. I take that to mean she liked it.

As the day wore on, it became less and less a normal day. The air was sultry, the kind that sits heavily on the shoulders and clogs the pores of the lungs. By noon, the sky darkened more surely than tempers. At three o'clock, the news anchor announced that a tornado had been sighted in our neighborhood but had not touched down. Eight miles from home, I worried about our house, about its inhabitants, even occasionally about the tomato crop. Co-workers kept assuring me that nothing had happened, and indeed when I tried to call home, I got a reassuring busy signal that meant Mother was occupied as ever on a weekday afternoon, chatting with Aunt Petty or Grandmaw.

But that evening when we stepped off the homeward bound bus, Donley and I met Carrington in her battered station wagon, all three of her toddlers standing sober-eyed in the front seat, and I knew my well-intentioned co-workers had told me false.

"Nobody's hurt." Carrington had the ability to cut right through to the heart of the matter. "At least not badly, or permanently, but the house..." A shrug completed the thought.

Shrugs are frightful things. They mean "No, you can't get out of traction yet" or "Might as well write off the car" or "I don't have a dime to pay back on the twenty dollars I owe you."

We didn't even bother to inquire what Carrington's shrug implied but rode silently the blocks to home. At first it didn't look so bad, except that the mulberry tree had moved closer to the house. No, the mulberry tree was on the house. And as we pulled around the back, there appeared to be lots more back yard than even we were accustomed to, because the wing that included Mother and Pop's bedroom and the back porch was gone, leaving that part of the cellar open to the sunshine that now shone apologetically on the pools of water that ran into the center of the uneven brick floor.

The barn still stood but looked disconsolate, as if it was waiting to be given a reason to remain upright. Down by the stream, the willow trees had re-draped their limbs sedately. Sheltered by the slope of the ground, they remained intact but their lone fellow survivor of all those magnificent trees was a redbud which, young enough to be limber, had bent with the wind but not broken.

Mother was displaying her pioneer spirit by boiling a teakettle over an outdoor fire. She had already set up a makeshift grill where she set a frying pan preparing to fix the evening meal. If I live to be as old as Moses, I will never forget and be inspired by my mother's indomitable courage. Yes, she had a nearly ungovernable temper and the rough side of her tongue could have given lessons to sandpaper, but none of that signified in the face of her ability to take disaster in stride.

"They had announced the all-clear," she told me when I put an arm around her, "when the roof flew off the barn over my head. I nearly panicked. Vala and Martin were down in the tomato field because there wasn't any warning."

"Are they all right?" At least Martin was all right, for I spotted him just then, picking through the debris, looking for something whole. "Where's Vala?"

Vala had gone into the house, armed with pitchers of rainwater, to wash her hair. Vala washed her hair as other women downed bracing cups of tea, but this seemed a little farfetched even for her.

"It was dirty," my mother explained, as if reading my mind. The tornado had lifted Vala from the north section of the field and sent her tumbling and rolling across the meadow, depositing her in the field to the east, just alongside the railroad tracks.

"And I had to walk all the way back," announced an aggrieved Vala, a towel covering her head, turban style.

"But Vala, you know how often you've been told to lie down if you are outside when a tornado hits."

"Lie down? Lie down?" Vala's voice was shrill. "I couldn't lie down in that muddy field. I was wearing my new jeans."

It was as if a tie had been cut, the old house as good as gone. As all of us worked to put together such pieces of our lives as could be salvaged, Luke was quietly married, and then in the same chronological order in which we had arrived, but even more quickly, Trent, Donley, and I married. Carter, Conner, Carrington, and Ragan had already established homes of their own.

The house plans underwent intensive redesign. We weren't the same family; we didn't need the same house

I study the photographs Laurel has brought me and drown in memory.

Chapter Twenty

The last two weeks of my down time were spent planning the party I would have, once the doctor resumed his less-than-important position in my life. I invited them all, my five brothers, my four sisters, all their children, and their children's children. We put up a tent in the backyard to make a place for them. The camera was ready, even the movie camera, and I prepared to take roll after roll of film. If ever I have to take to my bed again for more than an eight-hour stretch, I will have ready-made entertainment.

They all came and yet, looking around, I wondered. Where was the laughter we shared, the stories that made us giggle inappropriately but irrepressibly in church? Who were these sober-faced men who discussed annuities, actuarial tables, percentages of discounts, availability of funds? Where were Luke and Trent, Martin and Conner, Carter? And these attractive and well-groomed matrons, are they somebody I should know? Not Donley. Donley I would always recognize. My spirit still speaks to hers, and her children are only slightly less dear than my own. But what of these others who discuss returning to school as a solution to mid-life crisis, who speak of the chains of domesticity, but who at the drop of a garter button, break out pictures of the grandchildren—as if many of those children are not with us in the flesh at the same moment. I took the ice bucket to the refrigerator to fill it.

"It's not them. It's you." I hadn't seen my life's partner come up behind me. "You've been living too much in the past while you were laid up. You can't expect them all to be in tune with your thinking. None of them just spent seven weeks flat on their back, thirty years in the past."

I knew he was right, but it still saddened me. Was this the way it was with Pop, too? Had he been, as a youngster, as full of laughter and ill-advised schemes as we ourselves had been, and had ours died as our hair thinned and our teeth rotted? Poor Pop. I never in my life saw him laugh out loud and only about twice did I see a genuine smile on his lips. Had I known him when he was younger, would I have loved him more? Had he ever loved us? I don't know. He died without saying.

Memory is a prism. It catches the light of our laughter and shines it deeper hued on our sorrow and renders our grief less searing. In memory, the snowflakes fall without the cold smarting our eyes. Backward glances show us ourselves dancing through the rain, but block out the soggy shoes vainly set to dry over the heating stove.

St. Albert's had a church choir, but so did St. Ruth's, the small church with no parish, whose reason for existing was obscure and whose future was uncertain. I can forget the humiliation of being rejected for a choir position at St. Albert's because I remember the joy of practicing for Christmas at St. Ruth's. At St. Albert's, the choir lifted its voice in song, and the music soared. At. St. Ruth's, the music limped along accompanied by a wheezy organ. At St. Albert's, the choir practiced once a week, come spring rain or winter sleet. We who sang at St. Ruth's practiced diligently the week before Easter, and again the week before Christmas, and the newest hymn we sang was written by Martin Luther. But in memory, we sing as sweetly as the original Christmas choir.

All those years, as my sisters and my brothers and I were drowning our dollies, planting the fields, living out our juvenile lives, there were wars going on and our family was involved. First Carter, then Conner left home, yet the family circle still enclosed them. I remember the homecomings much better than I remember the tear-soaked departures.

We all of us married, some older, some younger, some for better, some for worse, some of us more than once. We grew up and raised families and became, each of us, respectable.

Still meditating on the mysteries of life, I descended to the laundry room to find the untapped store of ice cubes in the refrigerator there. I was halfway down the carpeted stair when I heard it, and I stopped instantly, ice cube bucket outstretched like a votive offering.

Had I conjured up the sound by wanting so badly to hear it or had it existed somewhere outside my brain? It came again. A giggle. I would know that lurching, throaty chuckle anywhere. My brother, Trent, must have descended the steps ahead of me, and down here waiting to surprise me, had found a remnant of his childish self to brighten my day. I could feel my face responding, growing a smile of its own.

"Did you see those pants my dad is wearing?" It wasn't Trent's voice at all. "What in hell is he thinking when he puts on striped pants and a flowered shirt? He calls them his golfing pants, and I guess he does scare the squirrels off the course."

The laughter rose and was subdued and broke out anew.

So here was where the children were, hiding out in the air conditioning and unless I missed my guess by a mile, making fun of their parents. Yes, I could hear my own Laurel, thrusting out words against the flow of her laughter.

"I swear…at least three hundred pictures. And all by herself, but laughing, or once she was crying. My brother had to go in once—didn't you, Dave?—to make sure she wasn't having some kind of attack. She laughed so hard she was wheezing…just her and all those pictures."

I will share a secret with you. Old is okay. You're wise, and at least to your face, your children respect you, and there's contentment when you look back on what you have achieved. But it's more fun to be young. It's more fun to make fun of your parents, than to have your children make fun of you.

How dared they? I almost dropped the ice bucket, giving me away. But then again, I knew how they dared. It was in their genes as surely as the sound of Trent's laughter could be heard when John opened his mouth and as surely as Donley's blue gaze looked out from her Mary's eyes. Here then, was the laughter I had been seeking. It hadn't died at all. It was just passed on. Safe with this generation and vigorous enough to last for ten or fifteen more.

Acknowledgments

My thanks to my nephew Steve Rakers, who formatted this book to make it more presentable.

To the *Liguorian Magazine*, which first published the Valentine story and gave permission for its inclusion in this book.

To Jennifer Maughan, who dealt wisely and well with my sentences, which went on and on and on, as well as with my computer illiteracy.

To my entire extended family, who possess such strong character and such a finely honed sense of humor that gave me material to draw on to create the characters.

About the Author

Helene O'Shea is regally tall, exquisitely thin, and cognizant of the latest styles—or maybe she isn't.

Still happily living in the same Midwestern city in which she was born and raised, she has an enviable husband and four entirely satisfactory grown children, and each of her grandchildren is a national treasure.

Ms. O'Shea is also fortunate to have any number of sisters, brothers, nieces, and nephews, all of whom are possessed of a healthy sense of humor, which is good.

Although this sounds like an obituary, she is almost certain that she is not dead—most days.